ENDORSEMENTS FOR

IT'S ALL ABOUT OBEDIENCE

It's All About Obedience describes the amazing journey of faith and obedience that Tim and Becky Keep traveled as God prepared them and later took them as missionaries from America to the Philippines. It is a brutally frank, part-testimony, part-confession, part-exhortation of their walk of obedience, sometimes exciting and rewarding and at other times painful and difficult. As a person who has traveled a similar road for the past twenty-eight years in Nigeria, I commend this book to all who want to know what missionary life is *really* like and to be challenged by it.

Dr. Danny McCain
Missionary Statesman, Founder and International Ambassador of Global Scholars

It's All About Obedience should be read by every serious Christian. Its lessons about the costs (and rewards) of true obedience, the importance of prayer, the challenge of living by faith, and the necessity of daily surrender will challenge and convict you. You will leave this book with a deeper appreciation for what it means to live in daily obedience and surrender to God.

Dr. Randall McElwain
Professor of Bible and Music, Hobe Sound Bible College

Becky has written *It's All About Obedience* in the "heart language" of a Christian seeking to walk life's pathway in obedience to Christ. She candidly wrote of human struggles and God's sufficiency. Her writing leaves the reader with hope – hope that anyone, regardless of their situation, can live a victorious, beautiful, and productive life through obedience to God.

Joy Budensiek
Author, Director of Intercultural Studies, Hobe Sound Bible College

Tim and Becky's lives are examples of faithful Christian workers who have served the Lord sincerely and devotedly. The stories in *It's All About Obedience* illustrate the victories and struggles of missionaries in our modern world. They share vignettes of the power of Jesus to overcome the various vicissitudes and many times serious difficulties that missionaries must face. I have known and followed the ministry of the Keeps for several years, and I feel that this book is a must-read for those who are interested in missions. It will feed your heart and mind. I highly recommend this book for all Christians. It will make you laugh, sometimes cry, but in the end you will rejoice with them.

Dr. Glen Reiff
Former missionary to Central America, Missionary Statesman

What a fascinating book that takes you beyond the "romance" and settles you firmly in the "reality" of missionary life. With a transparency that is at times painful, *It's All About Obedience* leads the reader through the real-life struggles of cross cultural ministry: from fear to faith, helplessness to hope, victim to victor, overcome to overcomer. The key, of course, is ***obedience.*** It is a book for every person interested in missions. From the prospective missionary to the prayer warrior at home, this will enlighten you to the true adventure of following God's call to foreign missions. Well done!

Rev. Steve Stetler
Missionary Field Director for Bible Methodist Missions, Mexico

Tim and Becky Keep have truly caught the essence of ministry. Whatever gifts and talents we bring to ministry are nothing without *obedience*. In this book, *It's All About Obedience,* Becky has given us insight into their journey of obedience as they ministered to others. It is a must-read!

Rev. G. Clair and Melba Sams
President for Heartland Conference, Bible Methodist Connection of Churches

This is Becky's book, but her husband, Tim, joins her in recounting events from their missionary life together. My wife and I laughed, teared up, felt frustrated, and identified with them over and over as we read. The overall theme is obedience, but the Keeps relate it to important missionary matters like culture shock, poverty, medical service, loneliness, and family needs. Read and enjoy! Read and be challenged to deeper levels of obedience!

Rev. Steve Hight
President, Evangelistic Faith Missions

As a missionary serving among the people described in this book, I get to see first-hand, every day, the enduring fruit of Tim and Becky's obedience to Christ. *It's All About Obedience* will make you laugh, cry, think, and pray – all within the space of a few short hours. I could hardly stop reading! It is theology poured out through lived experience – which I think is the best kind.

R. G. Hutchison
Missionary Field Director for Bible Methodist Missions, Philippines

Obedience does not come without struggles. Becky Keep, through her book, *It's All About Obedience,* beautifully depicts the Keep family's obedience. Becky has lovingly, humbly, and honestly laid out her heart's desire to obey God's call for their lives. Tim, Becky, and their children were a blessing to our own family during our time in the Philippines. We are truly grateful for God putting them in our lives at a time when we needed to be encouraged. Thank you Becky for writing *It's All About Obedience* and sharing your struggles, trials, thoughts, and triumphs. This book will be an encouragement to all who read it.

Colin and Terri Whittaker
Missionaries serving the Wesleyan Church in the Philippines

IT'S ALL ABOUT OBEDIENCE

ONE WOMAN'S DISCOVERY OF A FRUITFUL LIFE IN A FOREIGN LAND

IT'S ALL ABOUT OBEDIENCE

ONE WOMAN'S DISCOVERY OF A FRUITFUL LIFE IN A FOREIGN LAND

BECKY KEEP
WITH **TIM KEEP**

To our children,
with the earnest prayer that the stories contained in this book –
stories we have experienced together – will fuel your courage and
your passion for obedience to Christ and will help preserve your
heart for the Lord's soon return.

CONTENTS

FOREWORD

One of the most convicting scenes from the life and ministry of Jesus Christ is found in the Gospel of Mark:

> And a crowd was sitting around him, and they said to him, "Your mother and your brothers are outside, seeking you." And he answered them, "Who are my mother and my brothers?" And looking about at those who sat around him, he said, "Here are my mother and my brothers! For **whoever does the will of God, he is my brother and sister and mother**" (Mark 3:32-35, emphasis added).

The kinship of obedience to God is truly stronger than the ties of family. This is the relationship I have experienced with Tim and Becky Keep. From the very beginning days of their commitment to missionary service until this day, I have found them to be abandoned to God! The severest tests and attacks of Satan on them as very young missionaries did not deter them from obedience to God's call on their lives.

I knew the hardships and challenges the Keep family faced in getting to the mission field and the struggles to provide for the needs of their family after settling there because I was the treasurer of the missions organization they were working under. Yet, amazingly, God met their needs and gave them grace to endure the hardships. I saw firsthand the difficulties of living in the old dilapidated mission house (before another could be built) in the heat of the tropics. Yet they were gracious hosts and demonstrated a willingness to endure hardships. They had purposed to obey.

IT'S ALL ABOUT OBEDIENCE

When I became the Director of Missions for the Bible Methodist Connection of Churches, under which they served, I learned with even greater understanding just how agonizing and painful the realities of culture shock are and had deeper appreciation for the struggles of long separations from homeland and families. I will never forget Tim and Becky's sympathetic amusement as I struggled with a sense of depression while on long trips with them. They diagnosed me with a mild case of "culture shock"! I prayed harder for them afterward as the reality of those feelings remained fresh in my emotions for some time afterward.

Perhaps the greatest of the joys of my association with God's choicest servants, missionaries, has been the familial bonds formed as we truly became "family." What a delight it was to bring simple gifts from the homeland on my visits to the Keep family and the other missionaries. It warmed my heart more than I can say that the children began to call me "Uncle John" and were so excited to see me when I arrived. (I'm sure the suitcases full of little gifts had something to do with their joy!) I cherish the experience of watching the Keep children grow up and enthusiastically engage in ministry alongside their parents. Obedience inspires obedience!

So it is with tears brimming in my eyes and delight in my heart that I invite you to join me in sharing these accounts of the challenges and the victories of a missionary couple's life that has been used of God far beyond any of our comprehension in the whitened harvest fields. It is not about extraordinary people, however. It is about an extraordinary God and a couple who have discovered the rich rewards of living a life that is "all about obedience" to that extraordinary God! – Rev. John D. Parker

INTRODUCTION

*Nothing can wholly satisfy the life of Christ within his
followers except the adoption of Christ's purpose toward
the world he came to redeem....The men who are putting
everything into Christ's undertaking are getting out of life its
sweetest and most priceless rewards.*
J. Campbell White

Twenty years ago this spring Becky and I, along with our two
small children, were commissioned as missionaries to the
Philippine Islands. I was twenty-six and Becky was twenty-four. I
was insecure. Becky was fearful. And we could not have imagined
then how this commission would humble us, shape us, define us.

We could not have imagined the blessings that God would
pour out upon our family through the "adventures" of our thirteen
years of cross-cultural ministry together. We could not have imagined the disappointments we would endure, the grace we would
receive, nor the undeserved pleasures we would enjoy. We could
not have imagined the lives we would touch, the relationships
we would forge, the spiritual victories we would witness, nor the
thousands of physical needs that would be met through Becky's
medical ministry. We could not have anticipated the young men
and women we would *help* mentor, the nearly forty church plants
we would promote, nor the God-sized national vision we would
be privileged to encourage. We could not have imagined any of the
good that has come to us or through us because we did not, could
not, produce it. What we *could* do was obey.

IT'S ALL ABOUT OBEDIENCE

A fruitful life *in Jesus* isn't complicated; it's a matter of steadfast obedience!

I've been blessed with ministry which sometimes takes me to various countries around the world. In my travels I have met humble Christians who are making a tremendous impact for the kingdom of God in their families, clans, villages, and even whole regions. Most of them are poor with respect to material things. Many are not formally educated. Few have gifts or skills which measure up to contemporary standards of success. None are achieving true greatness through worldly wisdom, but through humble, Jesus-honoring obedience.

These brothers and sisters prove that you and I will impact generations not so much by trying to be, or do, something great, but by faith-filled obedience; that when we simply surrender to the sometimes rugged, rarely heroic, often humbling, mostly ordinary, always rewarded things which obedience to Christ demands, God will providentially place us and powerfully use us to affect a generation for eternity. That, in a nutshell, is the message of this book.

It's All About Obedience is written with two audiences in mind. The first audience is our own family. Becky and I have felt compelled to record the stories contained in this book for the sake of our children and grandchildren. We pray that this book will fuel their passion for obedience. You are the second audience. Our heartfelt longing that God would raise up a new generation of men and women who will "hate their lives in this world" for Jesus's sake, for the sake of his smile on their homes and churches, and for the sake of those yet unreached with the message of the gospel. Far too many "Christians" today are retreating from the hard things that true discipleship demands and therefore forfeiting more than they could ever dream.

Becky and I know how terrifying the steps of obedience can be, especially those first steps! In the following pages, you'll read some of our stories of fear and failure, faith and fulfillment as we began our journey. You'll read about our calling. You'll sit beside Becky on that first 747 bound for the Philippine Islands and hear the sound of metal as she buckles herself in for that first long flight.

You'll probably laugh at my culture-shock tears and at some of the funny experiences we've shared together as a family. We're sure you'll shake your head at some of our mistakes and then stand amazed, as we do, at God's power to redeem those mistakes for his glory. You'll travel with us into mountain villages as we share the hope of the gospel. You'll feel Satan's attacks, but then rejoice in the power of God's Word to defeat him.

In the pages that follow, you'll stand beside the bed of our sick children and celebrate God's healing power; join our missionary team in bringing Christmas peace to a very dark village on Christmas Eve; and, by the grace of God, you'll see God's kingdom grow in spite of human frailty and weakness. By the time you've read the last page, we hope you're more convinced than ever that Christian service is about obedience – not gifts, nor human cleverness, nor human perfection, nor human wisdom – but loving, enduring, sincere and child-like obedience.

It's all about obedience! Obedience in spite of fears. Obedience in spite of tears. Obedience graciously enabled. Obedience abundantly rewarded.

Tim Keep
February 2, 2016

CHAPTER ONE

It's All About Obedience

All God's giants have been weak men who did great things for God because they reckoned on his being with them.
Hudson Taylor

It was three years ago that I had the privilege of meeting Alma Hagan. We were attending a Christmas musical concert when a mutual friend said to me, "There is someone that I would like for you to meet."

She took me to where an elderly lady was sitting and introduced us. My friend explained that Alma and her husband had spent forty plus years as missionaries in northern India and Nepal. She then left us to get acquainted. I was immediately drawn to Alma's vivacious personality, bright smile, and her beautiful eyes that twinkled as she recounted their years on the mission field. Although her ninetieth birthday had come and gone, her mind was quick and alert. We only spoke for a few minutes, and I expressed regret that we couldn't sit down and have a long talk. I felt that she had so many things to teach me – things that I needed to learn. As I prepared to leave, I asked, "What was the key to your success and faithfulness for so many years?" Her answer was simple but powerful. She looked at me with a smile and a slight shrug of her shoulders and said simply, "It's all about obedience." As we said our goodbyes, she gave me a copy of her autobiography; and I walked away with those words, "It's all about obedience," ringing in my ears.

Alma's words struck a chord deep within me, and I heard them over and over again as I read her story. It was a story of a young couple's obedience in answering the call to take the gospel to the Hindu nation of Nepal. It was a story of that same young couple choosing to obey even when the door to Nepal was tightly closed and their mission seemed impossible. In Alma's own words she says, "When the door is slammed in your face, you can turn around and go home – or you can sit on the porch and pray and get ready for when it opens" (*When Nepal's Door Opened*, Prologue, p. v). They sat "on the porch" of a neighboring country for 20 years in simple obedience, working towards the day when that door would swing open. And swing open it did. A season of obedient waiting led to a season of abundant harvest.

I rejoiced to see the fruit of that obedience in Alma's life as she labored with her husband, cared for her four robust boys, and interceded for many. I watched in wonder as many were saved and the gospel made available in that spiritually dark country. The dominant thread woven throughout this woman's colorful life story was obedience. At every uncertain junction along life's path – and there were many – and in the face of each difficult circumstance, she chose to obey. At the end of the day, this is what a fruitful life of following Jesus is all about.

As I reflected on my own life as a wife, mother, missionary, nurse, and pastor's wife, the truth of Alma's words was brought into clear focus. It truly is "all about obedience." Although obedience has certainly not always provided a smooth and painless journey for our family, it has always somehow rendered the "next step" passable. There have been seasons when obedience has carried us on a garden path – pleasant and surrounded by beauty and blessing. On the day that our young son was diagnosed with cancer, that lovely path morphed suddenly and without warning into a steep hiking trail – one that left us often bruised and sore. There have been times when the footpath of obedience has appeared to our blighted vision to be overgrown with difficulty, and the temptation to vary our course just a bit to ease the journey has been strong. It was in those times, however, that looking forward on the path of obedience, we always found God's grace had cleared the path ahead just enough for us to carry on.

Before I take you further into our story, I would like to ask you to pause with me for a few moments and reflect on the implications of the following Scripture passages.

Therefore whoever hears these sayings of mine, and does them, I will liken him to a wise man who built his house on the rock: and the rain descended, the floods came, and the winds blew and beat on that house; and it did not fall, for it was founded on the rock. But everyone who hears these sayings of mine, and does not do them, will be like a foolish man who built his house on the sand: and the rain descended, the floods came, and the winds blew and beat on that house; and it fell. And great was its fall (Matthew 7:24-27).

Have you thought about the fact that obedience or disobedience to Jesus' teaching is the difference between the soul house that stands and the one that falls? The storms of life will batter every life sooner or later, and only those souls established by obedience will withstand.

Consider this word from the lips of Jesus:

Then he said to them all, "If anyone desires to come after me, let him deny himself, and take up his cross daily, and follow me. For whoever desires to save his life will lose it, but whoever loses his life for my sake will save it. For what profit is it to a man if he gains the whole world, and is himself destroyed or lost?" (Mark 8:23-25).

IT'S ALL ABOUT OBEDIENCE

Then Jesus said to those Jews who believed him, "If you abide in my word, you are my disciples indeed" (John 8:31).

The fundamental requirement for everyone who would follow Jesus is an unqualified obedience. I do not mean obedience which does not *stumble* or an obedience which does not *fail*, but obedience which ultimately prevails. A submissive, obedient walk with Jesus is the mark of every true disciple. Have you been tempted to believe that obedience in this thing or in that area is optional? Jesus never hides the price tag of a fruitful, fulfilling life.

Here is another sobering passage:

Then Samuel said: "Has the LORD as great delight in burnt offerings and sacrifices, as in obeying the voice of the LORD? Behold, to obey is better than sacrifice, and to heed than the fat of rams. For rebellion is as the sin of witchcraft, and stubbornness is as iniquity and idolatry. Because you have rejected the word of the LORD, he also has rejected you from being king" (1 Samuel 15:22-23).

Have you ever thought of how important full obedience is? Have you ever thought of a careless *heart* toward God's commands – willful disobedience – as "rebellion," "witchcraft," "stubbornness," "iniquity," and "idolatry"?! It ought to sober us to recall that Saul's *disobedient heart* – his stubborn rationalizations – became the flaw in his life which eventually robbed him of the kingdom and caused the Holy Spirit to depart from him (see also 1 Samuel 16:14).

To the obedient Jesus offers this amazing promise:

Most assuredly, I say to you, if anyone keeps my word he shall never see death (John 8:51).

Isn't it wonderful that Jesus offers this compelling promise of life for any person who commits to a life of obedience?

I found it interesting that my ninety-year-old friend, Alma, when asked what the secret to her success was, didn't list her educational achievements, personal fortitude, gifts, or talents. Instead, immediately and without pause, she had replied, "It's all about obedience." For on the tough days – days of loneliness, sickness, financial needs, family difficulties, and ministry doors seemingly slammed shut – it was a clear, defined choice to walk on in obedience that ultimately allowed God's purpose to be accomplished in their lives.

Lest you are tempted to now close this book thinking that perhaps it was written for those whom God will call to a far-away land, please read on. What I hope to convey in the following pages is a theme that can be applied to any life, anywhere. Whether your lot in life finds you living the exotic or the ordinary, there is a unique path of obedience just for you. Open your eyes and look around you. What is God asking of you today? Perhaps you are a college student and buried under the requirements of school and work. Maybe you're tempted to give less than your best and to be content with just sliding by. Or maybe you're a young mom who wearily wades through hours of domestic chaos each day in an effort to survive. You may be one who feels "trapped" in a job that is less than fulfilling and tempted to allow the mundane to rob you of a sense of purpose. Or perhaps you're now elderly and believe that your days of contributing anything of value to the world are over.

Whoever you may be and wherever life finds you today, I want to challenge you to embrace the place where God has planted you. Ask him to make you obedient to that place and its demands – to see it as a divine appointment and a place where you can experience great blessing and peace. Obedience to Christ in all of life's circumstances will determine your true success.

CHAPTER TWO

The Call to Relinquishment

*If a commission by an earthly king is considered an honor,
how can a commission by a heavenly King
be considered a sacrifice?*
David Livingstone

Tim and I, in our first pastoral assignment after Bible college, were about to discover this truth for ourselves. In January 1996, our third year of ministry, we found ourselves in the midst of one of the fiercest spiritual and emotional conflicts we had ever faced. It had been a tough month – a tough year, in fact.

While it was true that God had used this time to forge much-needed character in us, we were spiritually drained and needing some respite. In addition to this, **there was in both of us a growing restlessness which we couldn't understand**. Was God preparing us for something only he could see? Was there something he was about to do? An opportunity he was about to present? Was our present ministry about to come to an end? Without saying much to me at the time, Tim began to wonder if the Lord might be about to fulfill his dream for cross-cultural service … in the Philippine Islands. His belief that God had called him, us, to partner with national leaders in this country was born during a leadership conference during his junior year of Bible college. This is how he describes his calling:

> I'll never forget the night the Holy Spirit kindled the flame for the Philippines in my heart. During my junior year at Hobe Sound Bible College, Dr. Mike Avery, then Director of Bible Methodist Missions, came to challenge the student body toward full-time Christian service. In one of his evening messages, Dr. Avery shared the story of a Filipino pastor by the name of David Yucaddi. He spoke of pastor Yucaddi's powerful conversion to Christ from pagan darkness and of his call to spread the gospel among his Ifugao Tribe – a fierce, animistic tribe located throughout the Cordillera Mountain Range of Northern Luzon. Dr. Avery offered a vivid, compelling description of an evening when God knit his heart to David's as side-by-side they rode through the Philippine highlands *on top* of a dilapidated "Pinoy" (a locally made van of sorts). While they bumped and wound their way through steep mountain gorges and then climbed higher and higher toward the Ifugao town of Banaue, David had shared story after story of the gospel's power at work among his people, stories which would have fit beautifully within the book of Acts. Along with these stories, Dr. Avery explained that David had described his vision for a center where young men and women would be mentored and trained to take the gospel to the countless towns and villages throughout that region.
>
> While Dr. Avery spoke with passion about a man and a work I had never heard of, God began to do something in me that I find very hard to describe. Everything and everyone else in that room faded to the background; and in the stillness of my soul, I heard the voice of the Holy Spirit calling me. A fire began to burn inside my young heart – a yearning to be a part of what God was doing among that far off people group and to help this man named David fulfill his vision. **I remember thinking that it would be one of the highest honors I could possibly imagine if God would choose Becky and me for this ministry in the Philippine Islands.** My mind was so captivated that from

that night I took this desire as a promise. From that moment on, I began to pray that if the Lord was willing he would open the door for our family there. Yet even as I prayed, it seemed like such a long shot! Having no direct ties to Dr. Avery, his denomination, or this mission work, I had no idea how the Lord would get us there. That night I had to determine that if this call was truly from the Lord, then it was his responsibility to make the impossible possible. I would be ready when he opened the door, but I wouldn't open it or even turn the knob!

I never spoke of this "call" publicly and only rarely to Becky and a couple close friends. (Becky wasn't much for conversations about missions in those days!) As the months and years rolled by, I was sometimes tempted to doubt God's promise. At other times it surged like waves upon the shore of my mind, and I would imagine myself in the Philippines trekking over mountains through rice paddies sharing the gospel. **The promise was always a part of my prayer life even when all hope of fulfillment seemed absurd**. And then five years after the Lord promised, he fulfilled it in a most amazing way.

Around the end of January, Tim was feeling desperate to work through the restlessness and anxiety of his heart; and I knew he needed time alone with the Lord. Tim knew that I and our two small children would enjoy a break from the harsh Michigan winter, and so he volunteered to drive me to my parent's home about four hours away (we were a one car family). Spending a few days with Mom and Dad was always a treat! Besides, the freezing cold and snow had us housebound for so long that we all had a pretty severe case of "cabin fever." I was more than ready for this road trip to Indiana.

After dropping us off and spending a few minutes with Mom and Dad, Tim got back in his car and began his return trip. Little did we know what a turning point these four hours would be – not only for him, but our family and our future. Once again it will be best to let Tim share his part of the story:

IT'S ALL ABOUT OBEDIENCE

In January 1996 I found myself in an all or nothing tug-of-war with God. Here I was, a twenty-six-year-old pastor in my third year of ministry, and the devil had almost convinced me that I would never accomplish anything for God. I was in despair. I was confused. I felt restless. I felt trapped. For months I had carried such a weight on my chest that, honestly, at times I even wished to die; and recent pastoral challenges had only added to my pain. I remember driving Becky and our two children to her parents' home in Indiana so that they could enjoy a few days of rest and relaxation, and so that I could be alone with the Lord. I had to get some things settled with him. I spent almost the entire four hour drive home crying out to God like never before. And he spoke with me, too. Oh, how he met with me!

Somewhere around the third hour of that trip, the Holy Spirit gave me the grace to look heavenward and say, through a river of tears, "Father, I don't know what you have in store for Becky and me. I don't know if you want us to stay in the pastoral ministry or if you will ever open up that door to foreign missions for us. But, Father, I consecrate myself anew to you and to your perfect will, whatever and wherever it may be. I relinquish control, Father. If you want us to stay in our present assignment, I'm willing to stay if only you will give us staying grace and promise to bless us." And then I added, "But, Father, if you would fulfill your promise . . . if you would be pleased to call our family to the Philippines as missionaries, oh how grateful I would be." I think I kind of smiled on that one, not even half believing that he would do so anytime soon! I also promised the Lord that day that no matter how tempting it was, I would never try to open a door on my own but would trust in his power to align the hearts of men with his will. That night I slept as a man at peace, never dreaming that the Lord was already doing the aligning.

The event which unfolded the very next morning I consider one of the great miracles in our lives. Around 9:00 a.m. the phone rang and the current Missions Director for Bible Methodist Missions, Rev. Gary Brugger, was on the other end of the line. Keep in mind that we barely knew this man and had certainly never spoken with him before regarding my interest in missions, let alone Philippines missions. I held the phone tightly in my hand as he began. After a few pleasantries he simply said, "Tim, while driving home from a ministry trip out west yesterday, I began talking to the Lord about our need for a missionary family in the Philippine Islands. As I prayed, it seemed that the Lord brought you and Becky to my mind, and I knew I had to call you. Please, let me get right to the point: Tim, would you and Becky consider going to Philippines as missionaries?"

I nearly dropped the phone and knew instantly that this was God's answer to my relinquishment! I knew that this was a fulfillment of the promise he had given me on that night five years before. I answered Rev. Brugger with a quick, "We'll promise to pray about it," but when I got off the phone I was so overcome with joy that I literally danced like a man who had just hit the jackpot! I was a man released from prison! A bird set free! I felt like I had just been born again … again! I couldn't contain my joy and began to sing every song of praise I could think of to the God who fulfills promises and gives his children the desires of their heart. It wasn't until I called Becky that I settled down a bit.

On January 31, my peaceful, relaxing mini-vacation was interrupted by a most distressing phone call from Tim. After chatting for a few minutes about the kids, he suddenly said, "Becky, I received a phone call this morning from Gary Brugger." I was silent on the phone while he continued. "Becky, he asked me if we would be willing to consider going to the Philippines as missionaries." Although my husband's tone was calm and nonchalant, I knew him well and could hear the unmistakable, yet restrained, excitement in his voice. It was something that I had not heard from him for a very long time. I knew that he had been under a cloud of oppression for weeks. I had in recent days witnessed him seeking after God as I'd never seen him do before.

Now, I would love to continue here by writing of my sweet and positive response to Tim's news. The truth is, however, that **my heart was seized with fear, and if it could have spoken aloud would have thundered a resounding "NO!"** Instead, I blurted out, "Why in the world did you have to call and ruin my vacation?!" I can only imagine how deflated I left him feeling on that afternoon. He dropped the subject immediately; we talked for a few more minutes and ended the call.

After we hung up, I tried to resume a carefree day with Mom and Dad. It was futile. I could think of nothing but the terrifying possibility of leaving all that was familiar. I'm sure I had never looked for the Philippines on a map, much less considered taking my babies there to live. Surely this couldn't be the will of God for us. There were plenty of people more qualified than I. Plenty more willing. We were serving God and seeing people's lives changed right where we were, so why did we need to become foreign missionaries?

Most unsettling of all for me was the deep inner awareness, brought about by the Holy Spirit, that there was a part of me – a part of my heart and life – that I was holding in reserve. I really believed that my greatest desire was to serve, follow, and obey God; and it was deeply disconcerting to realize with that simple phone call that this might not be completely true. As I grappled with this, my mind was drawn to another day in my life when I had flashed God a yellow signal.

It was my freshman year of high school. One afternoon I was sitting in a study hall finishing up some homework. I had just come from chapel; my mind was still there, mulling over the things that I had heard. It had been a great chapel service. Our speaker had surrendered his whole life to God and had spent many years as a missionary in Bolivia. He had captivated us with creatively told stories of God's power, stories of danger, stories of humor. Most importantly, the missionary's love for God was so evident. There had been no altar call that I remember, no invitation to surrender one's life to God. It had been just another service, just another day at school. But as I sat there quietly reflecting on the things the missionary had said, I suddenly heard the voice of God speaking to my heart. "Becky," he spoke gently, "what if I called *you* to be a missionary?" I distinctly remember the emphasis being on *"you."* I felt myself drawing back in fearful reticence at the thought and couldn't shake it off. I spent the rest of the study hall unable to concentrate and attempting to convince myself that I hadn't really heard the voice of God. I reasoned that *surely it was only an impression brought on by a compelling missionary speaker!*

Time went by. I went on to finish high school, serving the Lord, but always with that little piece of me that lived in hesitation before God. I met Tim in my junior year. He was undoubtedly the man for me, and we were married in the fall after my high school graduation. While we had never talked about the possibility of missionary work, we both wanted to serve the Lord and had perfect peace about our relationship. I marvel at God's grace in bringing us together though we were so young, inexperienced, and unsure of what our future would hold.

It was less than one year after our wedding that Tim felt called to study for some kind of Christian ministry at Hobe Sound Bible College in South Florida. Since missions had never come up between the two of us, I assumed that he would study in the ministerial department, and this was his plan too. I knew that my place now was to follow my husband and believed that I was "off the hook" when it came to being a missionary. I was relieved to have that struggle behind me.

Halfway through Tim's freshman year, he came home from class one day with some startling news. "Honey," he said, "I just can't feel clear about joining the ministerial program. I feel certain that, for some reason, God wants me to join the missions department." My heart sank! There it was again – missions! I supported

Tim in this decision and never let on that **the mere word *missions* caused a tidal wave of anxiety to rise within me**. I pushed it down for, after all, Tim was only a freshman. A lot could change in the years to come, and it would be years before any kind of missionary work would become a reality in our lives anyway.

We continued with our education. I was enrolled at a local community college and received a degree as a licensed practical nurse. These were four years of our lives that God taught us many invaluable lessons about trusting in him to provide for our every need. We were surprised and blessed when God saw fit to give us a beautiful baby girl. Valerie was born right in the middle of Tim's sophomore year of college. She was born five weeks before I graduated from nursing school, and I returned to school when she was only ten days old.

Tim became skilled in multi-tasking during those college days. I worked the evening shift; and he cared for Valerie while studying, researching, and writing papers at the same time. I don't know how he pulled it off, carrying her to the library night after night. Many nights he would study while lying on the living room floor as Valerie happily crawled all over him. He was so wonderful with her, and I loved knowing that she was with Daddy while Mommy worked. I often had trouble getting her to sleep on my nights off and must admit that it annoyed me just a little to have him tell me what I was doing wrong.

Tim and I had to be creative in finding ways to connect with one another. Because we worked opposite shifts, time together was a rare treat. We tried to squeeze in a date night every week, which usually consisted of a milkshake at the local Denny's. For two college kids with a baby in tow, this was about all our budget could handle.

I was delighted when we received an invitation to pastor a small church in Western Michigan just before Tim graduated from college. Perhaps this would be God's "mission field" for us.

THE CALL TO RELINQUISHMENT

We loaded our U-Haul trailer and bid goodbye to Hobe Sound only two days after graduation.

Three years had gone so quickly. We had witnessed lives changed. God had blessed us with a sweet baby boy, Timothy Jr., in May of 1994. Sure, we had had our share of disappointments, but God had never failed to show himself faithful during these years.

After the phone call from Tim, I could no longer push God away. I could no longer ignore his firm yet gentle voice beckoning me to acknowledge his call. I had heard all of my life that "God's way is the best way," and that, "He would never leave you where his grace could not keep you." I had been told since infancy, by godly parents, that my life was not my own; that I had been brought into this world for a purpose; that God had a wonderful work for me to do. I knew that I had been dedicated to God as a tiny baby, and that my parents had fully and completely entrusted my life to the Father.

Though I understood with perfect clarity the choice that was mine, my mind wrestled with the ramifications of that choice. *What if God's way didn't turn out to be "best"? What if I were called to suffer, to lose a child, to live in poverty and obscurity, or even to die? Would his grace keep me then?* **My flesh cried out for comfort, familiarity, and ease.** I knew that yielding to God meant a complete and total relinquishment of every detail of my existence. I would have to renounce my claim on my rights, my life, my children, my husband, my future. **I knew that this was not a tentative, "dipping one's toe in the water" moment for me. It was, rather, a plunging into the deep unknown of God's sovereign will.** This was all or nothing! My mind was illuminated with the truth that despite my godly upbringing and faithful parental training, my parents couldn't make this choice for me. I could follow my husband to the end of the earth out of rigid duty, but even that would not – could not – destroy the hidden barriers in my heart, the barriers that I knew would render me powerless, barren, and cold. I was at a crossroads, and this crossroads was mine alone!

For two weeks Tim remained silent on the matter. There were no persuasive arguments. No guilt trips. No pressure. He was given vast amounts of divine wisdom in dealing with this reluctant wife. And while my husband was quiet – perhaps *because* he was quiet – the Holy Spirit was doing his convicting work in my heart. As I began to listen – really listen to his most patient voice, the mist of confusion brought about by my own self-deception began to clear. I saw that I could continue with dogged determination the pursuit of what I wanted. But I was also made aware, by the power of the Holy Spirit, of the dreadful disillusionment that would most certainly follow disobedience. On the other hand, I glimpsed the beautiful path of peace which would be mine were I to choose the simple, though not easy, path of obedience. I longed for peace. I was tired of trying to create my own reality. On February 17, 1996, I simply laid down my will and accepted God's plan for my life, our lives.

With that decision a calm restfulness possessed me. With the cessation of war came tranquility, contentment, and even a joyful anticipation of the future. With surrender came certainty, certainty that my heavenly Father would take each step of this daunting journey with me. It would be his strength, his wisdom, his purity, his power that would enable me to "take up my cross, and follow Jesus."

For years I have spoken on different occasions of my "struggle" with answering God's call on my life, the struggle for complete relinquishment. It was easy to talk about when I used the word "struggle." Somehow, the word "struggle" sounded rather . . . innocent. After all, it's *normal* to *struggle* with the enormity of such a decision, isn't it?

Some time ago, however, while listening to the late Elisabeth Elliot on a rerun of her radio program, *Gateway to Joy*, I heard her say that the word "struggle" simply means for many of us "delayed obedience." I realized that she was right; and that while we can frame it however we like, there is nothing innocent about delaying obedience to the one who created us, suffered and died for us, and redeemed us. Surely he has every right to make demands upon our lives.

Should it not be our highest privilege as his children to relinquish our rights – not tentatively, or cautiously – but with reckless abandon to his call? And yet, with all of his power and rights as our Father and Creator, he doesn't exercise his right by beating us into submission. Rather, he lovingly deals with us, sometimes through long and circuitous routes, bringing us to a place of willing relinquishment. And what blessings follow those children who make that choice. For every act of obedience, there is a blessing. For every moment of suffering, there is solace. **For every sacrifice, there is a Savior who never stops giving of himself to those who obey him**.

As we wrap up this chapter I would like to ask you to reflect on a pretty hard-hitting biblical passage which calls every true disciple to total relinquishment:

> *If anyone comes to me and does not hate his father and mother, wife and children, brothers and sisters, yes, and his own life also, he cannot be my disciple. . . . So likewise, whoever of you does not forsake all that he has cannot be my disciple* (Luke 14:26, 33).

Perhaps like Tim you need to say "yes" to the *present*. You may need to say an unqualified "yes" to humble service, to humble people, in a humiliating place. You may need to say "yes" to a season of drudgery, a season of pain, or a season of waiting . . . for a harvest of joy!

Perhaps like me you need to say "yes" to God's *call*. You may need to say "yes" to the unknown, to discomfort, or to fearful prospects. You may need to be made willing to face your fears for the sake of those who are perishing without the knowledge of the gospel. You may need to be made willing to suffer others to save. Your "yes" is a "yes" to the surpassing pleasure awaiting those who lay down their gifts and treasures at the feet of Jesus.

Others of you may need to say "yes" to God's *time*. As Tim discovered, God's promises will be fulfilled, but only in his time. One cannot rush the plans of the Almighty, and to attempt to pull God toward our agenda is an exhausting affair. Great missionary statesman E. Stanley Jones reminds us of this with this compelling illustration: "If I throw out a boat hook from the boat and catch hold of the shore and pull, do I pull the shore to me, or do I pull myself to the shore? Prayer is not pulling God to my will, but aligning my will to the will of God." What a good word for those who tire of waiting.

Some who read this may need to say "yes" to God's *good*. Satan has convinced many believers today that anything good and delightful must not be from God, whose ways are always demanding and hard. When German pastor Dietrich Bonhoeffer was criticized for planning to marry during a time of war, he said to his critics, "Our yes to God is a yes to the good things he has created. God's good creation must be enjoyed."

Jesus follows his call to relinquishment with an amazing promise:

> *He who finds his life will lose it, and he **who loses his life for my sake, will find it*** (Matthew 10:39, emphasis added).

CHAPTER THREE

The Fear Factor

God isn't looking for people of great faith, but for individuals ready to follow him.
Hudson Taylor

Fear is a natural emotion; but acting on fear, rather than faith, is a form of rebellion – rebellion which could lead to a life of aimless wandering.

Just ask the Israelites. After listening to the report of "giants" in the land of promise, they shook in their sandals! Numbers 14 describes how they wept with fright as they imagined their children becoming prey for the barbaric natives of Canaan. *"We should have died in the land of Egypt,"* they moaned, reminding us that it is natural to prefer the familiar to the foreign even when the familiar is a life of bondage. Choosing fear over faith, Israel stubbornly refused to take the risk.

Joshua and Caleb pled with the people to reconsider: *"If the Lord delights in us, then he will bring us into this land ... a land flowing with milk and honey. Only do not rebel against the Lord, or fear the people of the land, for they are our bread; their protection has departed from them, and the Lord is with us. Do not fear"* (Numbers 14:8-9). Israel refused the opportunity. Referring to this story, Dennis Kinlaw states, "The sadness of the story still grips the reader. How true to life it is. There is a 'tide in the affairs of men' that if seized leads to greatness. If it is missed, one is left to wander. Opportunities do not stand waiting at the door" (Dennis Kinlaw, *This Day with the Master*, March 1).

While my relinquishment to God's call on that cold February day was truly sincere and complete, I found that it did not free me from all anxiety toward the unknown. And though my initial surrender to God's call was foundational, it wasn't necessarily the most difficult. In obedience I had stepped through God's open door. Obedience had taken me over a decisive threshold where a new journey would begin, in an amazing new "world." This new "world" was a sure destination from God's perspective, but to get there I had to travel unfamiliar roads.

This journey was one which would require a million and one tiny daily deaths to myself – each equally excruciating. I discovered that each piece of furniture, each personal item, each accumulated "thing" that I had to let go of in order to take hold of this new opportunity represented a small death – a letting go of "me." Tim began to feel the weight of his responsibilities to uproot and replant his family in a strange country; he struggled with anxiety too. I was astonished at how painful the process was. It was as if with every passing day we were confronted with fresh opportunities to abdicate our rights and renounce control. As we daily offered up even the tiniest bits of our lives to God in trembling obedience, we felt his steady hand, his loving gaze, and most importantly his strength compelling us to pursue this road of relinquishment.

Tim was twenty-six and I was twenty-four when we started this new journey of obedience. We were young, had two small children, and no missionary experience. When we boarded that plane on the morning of October 17, 1996, nothing could have prepared me for the internal firestorm of emotions that I experienced. Tim and I hugged and hugged again our parents, siblings, and friends who had come to bid us farewell. Valerie and Timothy got lots of kisses. Someone led out in a departing hymn, which rather added to the solemnity and gravity of this moment! Then we resolutely walked the down the jetway as if it were a gangplank, boarded the plane, and settled the children in their seats. I turned to buckle myself in and distinctly remember the cold "click" of the seatbelt. Then, it was the sound of finality; but, as I think of it now, it was also the sound of a resolved soul buckling itself to the will of God and steeling itself for the storms which often accompany those first steps of obedience. I sat back and thought, *This is it, I'm all in. There's no turning back now. When this plane lands, I'll be nearly ten thousand miles away from everything that I've ever known.*

I found out rather quickly that it wasn't the big picture of what God had asked of me that overwhelmed me. I had settled that! I had made a choice to follow God. I knew in my head that duty came before delight, and my deepest desire was to obey. It was, rather, the natural things, the fleshing out of that obedience in the details of my new assignment that threatened to derail my obedience, weaken my faith, and render me faint and feeble in my pursuit of God.

Obedience didn't hinder Satan from using all of his clever tactics to erode our faith. His greatest weapon against us was fear. For me it began when we were traveling from the airport up to our home in the town of Villasis. We had stopped at a travel plaza to refuel the vehicle and use the facilities. I took Timothy Jr. with me into the ladies' restroom and was horrified when a strange Filipino lady walked in, exclaimed loudly over this "cute Americano," took my two-year-old little boy's face in her hands and kissed him on the mouth! **My inability to protect my kids in this "strange" land with its "strange" people terrified me.** *My son could have just contacted tuberculosis from this lady,* I thought. After all, this was a country where, according to some experts, up to one-third of the population could be carrying the disease. I was visibly shaken after coming out of the restroom and relayed the incident to

Tim. He laughed and shrugged it off, but I didn't to see any humor in it at all.

A few days later, we were back in Manila to begin our paperwork for visas. While there, we decided to visit a mall just a short distance from our guest house. After a nice dinner in the mall, Rev. Gary Brugger, who accompanied us to the Philippines and stayed with us for the first three weeks, decided to get us a couple of "taxis" for the drive back to the guest house. These were not your ordinary taxis. Filipino's called them "pedicabs," but they were nothing more than a bicycle with an attached sidecar. I'm not sure how it happened, but I ended up alone in one pedicab with Valerie, five, and Tim Jr., two. Tim and Gary were in the pedicab behind us. What an absolutely hair-raising ride! I can still close my eyes and hear the creaking of the wheels and feel the jerking motion of the rickety frame of the cab as the driver turned this way and that, dodging cars, buses, and motorcycles.

As if this wasn't alarming enough, when the pedicab came to a stop I was doubly alarmed to find that we were sitting in the middle of a huge intersection with what appeared to be hundreds of noisy, fast-moving, horn-blowing vehicles belching noxious diesel fumes all around us. With sweaty palms and a knot in my stomach, I clutched my children, both of whom were oblivious to the danger we were in. In that moment of panic, I had one thought: *I've got to get out of this contraption.* Before I could act, the cab began to roll forward again. Without giving common sense a chance to kick in, I grabbed both kids firmly and jumped out! The driver turned around and looked at me with a stunned expression; but because he was already in the middle of traffic, he couldn't stop. **When I heard Tim yelling frantically from behind me, I realized what a stupid thing I had done!** I had removed myself and my children from a disturbing, but relatively safe situation, into a most dreadful one! There we stood in the middle of moving traffic, and in a much more perilous place, all because of the demon of fear. Thank heavens, Tim and Gary quickly jumped out of their pedicab to get us across that crazy intersection to safety. How foolish it was to think that I knew better than the pedicab driver for whom such circumstances were native, better than one who had crossed this way hundreds of times. Natural instincts can be deadly in a land where everything is foreign. Survival for the obedient believer depends on trust.

I wasn't the only one struggling to maintain a sense of equilibrium in this foreign place, as you'll soon discover. We moved into the mission house on the campus of the Bible college where Tim would be teaching. The yellow, wood framed house was more than fifty years old and set about three feet off the ground on about a dozen concrete pillars. The floors were wooden, too, but had no sub-flooring, which meant that there wasn't much separating us from the damp ground (and "critters") below! The holes in the floor in several of the rooms were a bit discomforting to us. We didn't even want to think about what might be lurking down there, just waiting to crawl into our house. (Later, a nest of cobras was found under this house.)

The first order of business, Tim and I decided, was to cover the dark brown walls with something brighter and to freshen the place up a bit. Rev. Lauro Forto, our Filipino Bible college president, assured us that some of the male students were competent painters and that they would be thrilled to earn a few pesos by helping us paint. We purchased the paint and welcomed four smiling young men – Francis, Edward, Onci, and June – into our home to begin the work. Tim gave them careful instructions and some old sheets for drop cloths. **With every instruction they smiled broadly, shook their heads confidently, and said, "Yes, sir! Yes, sir!"** Feeling that all was well, we left them to their work and went to do some shopping at the market.

Returning to the campus a few hours later, we found the students happily painting; but I watched the blood drain from Tim's face as he took in the scene before us. All three young men were using our wooden dining room table as a ladder to reach the ceiling, and their white footprints were all over the top! There was paint splattered over the floor, the piano, and just about every other surface in the room it seemed! There was not a drop cloth to be seen anywhere, probably because they didn't want to ruin a still usable sheet. When Francis noticed Tim's dismay, he smiled and assured him, "Don't worry, sir, we will clean it up with paint thinner." And they did. Now, we not only had a freshly painted house, but freshly stripped floors and furniture!

Tim and I both laugh now retelling this story; but, regrettably, we didn't see the humor in it then. I'll never forget being awakened at three o'clock the next morning by a very strange noise coming from the other side of the bed. *What is that?* And then it slowly dawned on me that my husband – this strong, capable man lying in the bed beside me – was shaking with sobs! "Honey, what's wrong?" I asked. "Becky," he replied through his tears, "how am I going to teach these guys systematic theology when I can't even teach them how to paint my house!?" The enormity of the task which lay before Tim had completely washed away all confidence and filled him with fear.

We lay there in the darkness, on a lumpy old mattress, feeling miserable. Our inner turmoil, combined with the stifling heat, an old rattling ceiling fan above us, and the roosters *already* crowing incessantly just outside our window, all blended together in one cacophony of brutal reminders that we were so very far from life as we had always known it. In those lonely early morning hours, we felt like a couple of frightened grade-schoolers away from home for the first time. We thought, silently at first and then aloud, *God, are you sure that you knew what you were doing when you called us here? Surely there were others far more qualified and adventurous than we are!* Then, we did the only thing we knew to do; we joined hands and talked to our Father. We reminded him of how weak and frightened we felt, how impossible this assignment was, and how dependent we were on his strength. We may have prayed for other things, too; but what we remember is that we just cried out to the Lord in desperation, reminding him of his word. We reminded him also that we were here in obedience to his calling and that he *must* help us! Our burdens certainly didn't just roll away that night, but our faith did secure a fresh hold on his promises.

Tim remembers well another time in our first few weeks on the field when he found himself reduced to tears:

> We didn't have a telephone or internet access on campus in the mid-nineties; so if we wanted to make contact with our family in the United States, we'd have to find an old-fashioned call center. These were cramped, stiflingly-hot little offices just off the street where a bored-looking operator would dial one's phone number for them. After a connection was made, one would be assigned to a particular phone booth along the wall. One day, after finishing up some business in Carmen (a village next to ours), I felt so lonely to hear a voice from home that I stepped into one of these places and asked the operator to call my parents. Mom answered and her voice sounded like the voice of an angel. I tried to have a conversation, but before I could say more than a sentence or two I got too choked up to continue. Embarrassed, I just hung up, hoping she would think we got disconnected. Culture shock can reduce a man to a boy in a hurry!

Our feelings of helplessness, loneliness, and fear wouldn't go away for a very long time; but in spite of our weakness, the Lord heard and answered our cry for help. In fact, as Tim and I look back on those days, already twenty years behind us, we are truly amazed by the opportunities he placed before us, opportunities to impact his kingdom in significant ways. Tim not only became a teacher but also a mentor to most of his students. **At least six of the feet which tracked paint across our table on our second full**

day as missionaries have become "beautiful feet" spreading the gospel across the mountains and valleys of the Philippines. It is those very feet, in fact, that are responsible for at least seven new church plants and many, many souls.

Indeed, it encourages us to realize that a number of the students Tim was privileged to *help* train that first year are men and women of real stature in the Philippine work today. Some are pastors and pastor's wives. Two of the young men have become national church leaders. One is a teacher in the Shepherd's College. One is in heaven, but she left a wonderful testimony of love for her Savior and a new church she helped her husband plant. We would not exaggerate our role in any of this success. We do want to be reminded, however, that in weakness we become strong when we rest in God's all-sufficient grace. Truly God doesn't need our gifts and confidence, but rather our brokenness and trust.

At every turn it seemed there was something large and looming which induced fear in me, but nothing frightened me more in those first months than driving Filipino highways. I realized with that first ride in the pedicab that transportation was going to be something of a challenge. It appeared to me that everyone on the road wrote their own rules.

We inherited a rather dilapidated jeep from the previous missionaries. With a bit of trepidation, Tim began driving it around town until he gradually learned how to weave and dodge his way along. It was common to have to stop for cows, goats, chickens, dogs, and even small children in the road. Because Filipinos had a "thing" for passing on blind curves, even on two lane roads, it was unnerving to look up and see a large bus or truck bearing down on us head on. Just when we thought it was game over, the bus driver would swerve back into his lane. Many times we had to swerve off the road to avoid a head-on collision. I became convinced that these road trips would be my demise and could picture myself lying in a casket with the word "Isuzu" (most common trucks on the road there) permanently stamped on my forehead. I developed a pretty severe case of "road rage" and an absolute aversion to traveling. I even told Tim on one occasion, "If I can't walk, then I'm not going!" I became an expert "backseat driver, prayer warrior, and bundle of nerves" each time we got into the car. I'm sure it was miserable for Tim to have to drive with me along.

I didn't realize how *my* fear was affecting my children until one day. . .

On one of our excursions into town, Tim stopped to go into a place of business while the kids and I remained in the jeep. Tim Jr., then two years old, immediately jumped into the driver's seat. "Mommy," he said, "let's pretend like I'm Daddy, and I'm the driver. Where do you want to go?" Deciding to play along, I said, "Let's go to Grandma's." "Okay," he said. He looked at me with an excited grin. He was adorable with his cheeks flushed from the sweltering heat and his hair lying in damp, sweaty curls around his face. He began bouncing up and down on the seat, turning the steering wheel, honking his horn, screeching his brakes, and making loud driving noises. I sat quietly, enjoying his enthusiasm. Suddenly he turned to me, **"Come on, Mommy," he called impatiently, "do what you're supposed to do!"** With a questioning look I asked, "What am I supposed to be doing, son?" "You know, Mommy, you're supposed to say, 'Oh, God!. . . Oh Jesus!. . . Please help us!'" he said. I laughed out loud, but it sobered me to think that I had made such an impression on him with my uncontrolled fear.

I realize now that my fearful responses were a subtle way to retain some control. I had obeyed God in coming to this place; I had given up my own desires and wishes for his; I had relinquished my rights to my life; but I found it very difficult to open my hands and release my fears. *After all, isn't it my vigilant responses to fear and my pro-action which keep me and my children safe in this dangerous land?* I thought.

I can identify with the Israelites and their "grasshopper" mentality as they wavered between fear and faith. Can't you? As floodwaters rushing into a peaceful village, destroying everything in their path, fear often threatened to destroy my vitality and productivity. I felt as though I was drowning in fear – fear of food, traffic, disease, thugs, you name it. Were it not for grace, I, too, could have chosen aimless wandering in a familiar but barren desert. Were it not for God's mercy, I, too, would have turned away from a land flowing with blessings – blessings veiled by intimidating giants.

Although I didn't cease being afraid in a moment of time, I did choose obedience. I chose God's Word over fear's threats. I sided with a reliable God against my unreliable emotions. I learned to confess every fearful response as sin. These choices were the keys which gave me access to God's promises; and they will be the keys for you, too. While my fears were natural and some even well-founded, they were becoming sin in my life. By giving them such a place of prominence, I was subtly sweeping Christ and his Lordship off of the throne of my heart and mind. I found it impossible for me to *act* in faith when so often *reacting* in fear.

Fear is the greatest threat to a fruitful life. Fear can be debilitating, especially an unhealthy fear of God. Such fear can wrap its tentacles around our hearts and suffocate our vitality. Tim and I believe that fear is at the heart of most disobedience, and that at the heart of most of our fears is a lack of confidence in the goodness and trustworthiness of God. *Can his truth and judgments really be counted on? Does he have my best interest at heart?*

Our natural instinct, I think, is to hold on tightly to what feels comfortable and familiar to us and to build "protective" walls around ourselves and our families, walls which offer illusions of safety. I say illusions because the emotional and spiritual walls we

build are never secure enough. The trials of life will, sooner or later, pour through the gaps in our fortifications.

I encourage you to overcome fear by cultivating faith in a faithful God and by putting him to the test. Our God is a living God, and he loves to show up in every detail of our lives.

Is God putting something before you right now? A new opportunity? A new ministry? A new relationship? Are you intimidated by all that could go wrong? Don't let fear paralyze you. The land ahead will be challenging; but it will also be a land of victory, joy, and plenty. In contrast, the land of fear's consequence will be a land of aimless wandering.

When we remember that our success depends on his strength, his power, his ability, his protection, we can face our fears and move forward with our confidence placed firmly where it belongs.

CHAPTER 4

Dodging Disillusionment

Tell the students to give up their small ambitions and come eastward to preach the gospel of Christ.
**Francis Xavier, missionary to India,
the Philippines, and Japan**

The unspeakably joyful substance God will lavish on the obedient will far surpass any dreamy, romantic *fantasies* he may have had!

One afternoon about three months into our new life in the Philippines, I found myself standing in our front yard, staring wistfully into the blue sky above me. I had run out of our house after hearing the faint but unmistakable roar of a jet plane. As I stood there watching the plane etch a white line across the sky, an intense longing swept over me. Oh, how I longed to be on that plane headed somewhere, *anywhere*!

My feelings that day can be summed up with this journal entry that I found recently – one which I had written just days before seeing that airplane: "*Here I am, ten thousand miles from home, totally inadequate for the job.*" Like so many other first-time missionaries, I was suffering from wrong expectations about what my life as a missionary would look like. I had envisioned work and ministry that was always rewarding, challenging, and people based. I could easily have imagined myself spending tranquil, sun-bathed afternoons sitting under a mango tree sharing the Bible with adoring, half-naked natives! I had dreamed of practicing my nursing skills and making a tremendous difference in people's lives. *I mean, this is what missionaries do, right!?*

Tim laughs now at the romantic notions he once held. In the months leading up to our departure for the Philippines, he imag-ined himself preparing lectures while sitting thoughtfully at a rustic desk in a bamboo office: Bible open, breeze blowing softly through windows opening to a tropical paradise, eager students awaiting his "revelations"! While we did live on a beautiful, trop-ical campus covered with Acacia, palm, and mango trees, it never felt quite as romantic as he had hoped.

You may smile at our naivety, and I know that I've exaggerated a bit; but in truth, nothing could have prepared us for the *reality* of missionary life. I found that very little of what consumed each of my days *seemed* to have any redemptive quality at all. I was totally unprepared for the endless cycle of minutiae which occupied near-ly every waking moment. Not only was I *not* engaged in much of what I would have called "ministry"; but the daily tasks of cooking, laundry, grocery shopping, and caring for my husband and two small children left me feeling inept and frustrated. I wasn't even doing these tasks well.

I remember the old washing machine that sat in my kitchen. It only worked about fifty percent of the time; and yet, I was de-termined to deal with my own laundry. The Filipinos were so kind and willing to help me, but I was too proud to even think of asking someone to wash my clothes. Anyway, I had watched them each afternoon as they washed their clothes using the hand pump locat-ed at the center of our campus. It looked easy enough. They would sit for hours methodically scrubbing, rinsing, and wringing each piece of laundry. Their smooth brown arms, seemingly tireless, moved fluidly and efficiently. It looked effortless. *I can do this!* I thought. I remember the day I gathered all of our laundry together and carried it with determination to the back porch. Valerie was so excited to "wash clothes like the Filipinos." We sat on small stools and began our task.

Less than an hour later I looked down at my sore and bleeding knuckles. My arms were aching with exhaustion. My back and legs screamed for mercy. With a deflated sigh, I wearily picked up the still very full basket of laundry and called it quits. Defeated, I swallowed my pride and accepted help.

I approached my stove each evening with fear and trembling. It had to be lit manually. I was terrified of it, especially after a small explosion had knocked pictures off the wall and singed my eyebrows.

I remember my first trip to the market to buy food. We walked through the market in the oppressive heat. My stomach rolled as I viewed the tables laden with freshly-butchered meat. The "Suki's" (meat sellers) were waving long duster brooms over the meat to keep the many flies from settling for too long. The smells assaulted my senses, and I discreetly covered my nose and mouth as I watched the blood running off the tables and onto the floor beneath. I recoiled at the mere thought of feeding this to my family. We found a supermarket, and I was delighted to find some cans of Spam. I had never really cared for it before, but that day it had the appeal of filet mignon. After a couple of weeks of Spam dinners, my family tired of it. It was then that we providentially met some wonderful veteran missionaries: Dr. Bob and Kay Bickert and Dr. Paul and Jan Turner. They assured me that the meat was good and kindly instructed me on when and how to buy it and how to properly clean and prepare it. I was grateful and took the advice of these dear people who had lived overseas for many, many years and who still appeared to be healthy and fit.

Having to exert so much energy on every detail of life, even the most mundane, caused me to live "on edge." The ease with which I had cared for my family back in the US was only a wistful memory. Everything here was so difficult. I found myself defeated and, honestly, quite grumpy at the end of most days.

Some of you reading may be shocked at my forthrightness in this chapter. I know now what I wish I had known then. I had heard *about* culture shock. I had heard that adjusting to a new culture, country, food, and way of life could sometimes be brutal. But, I somehow never made the connection between what I was experiencing and culture shock. I was certain that I was just a "bad" missionary.

I began reading biographies of great missionaries; but because I read them through the murky lens of my own failure, I was left feeling conscience-stricken by their success stories. These stories seemed to confirm the dismal thought in my mind that *I was no Betty Stam. My poor husband has made a dreadful mistake and married the wrong woman.* I know that my perspective was skewed, but it seemed as if these people whom I read about were so much more ardent and selfless in their pursuit of God and his call on their lives. I wondered, *Did they ever wake up feeling the darkness of defeat? Did they ever long for home?* I had mistakenly believed, subconsciously I'm sure, that surrender to God's will would somehow trigger an automatic love for every aspect of what he had asked of me, that I would somehow just fit effortlessly into this new life.

Previous to this time in my life, I had been confident in my ability to cope and flex with whatever came my way. **I was a middle child born into a family of nine children and had never been spoiled or coddled.** I had always been trained to get along with people, to be thankful for what I had, to eat what was set before me, and to love and obey God. I realized, however, in this sea of change, that I had radically overestimated my capacity to manage. I was in way over my head and drowning.

DODGING DISILLUSIONMENT

God so lovingly ministered to me through my husband who prayed tirelessly with me and for me: never judging, never condemning, always loving. This will be a good place to let Tim share *his* side of *my* struggle:

I realized that if we were going to make it through this unbelievably difficult culture shock, and make this land our home, we were going to have to depend moment by moment on the Lord. I spent a lot of time on my face (literally) in those early days, especially on behalf of Becky, for whom the adjustments were far more difficult than for me. I can still smell the wood floor of my tiny office where I'd often disappear throughout the day. And, if I pause just a moment, I can still hear the sounds of laughter and Ilocano chatter, the clucking of chickens as they scratched for food, and the distant "squeeeeak" of the water pump handle as students pumped wash water into basins. These sounds, drifting through the opened windows as I prayed, simply reminded me of how far from "home" we were. How comforting they are *now* ... but *then* these sounds often increased my loneliness.

At other times, after we had tucked the children in bed at night, I'd walk around and around the campus with Becky's *"Tim, I just can't do this!"* ringing in my ears. On those countless walks, I would find myself praying in desperation for God to relieve the pressures and tensions we were under, to forgive my impatience, and to fuel our endurance as a couple and family. I reminded him over and over again that he would have to touch Becky's heart and mind or we couldn't possibly stay in this country, and that the power of miracles was his alone. On my office floor and on those evening walks, I learned that bearing one another's burdens – rather than the judgment I was prone to render – is the fulfillment of the law of Christ. I also learned that our greatest struggles can only be settled through childlike, earnest, persevering prayer. There were no magic moments of adjustment for Becky and me. Our day of deliverance dawned slowly. By the end of our first year the sun was beginning to rise, though there were many moments of pleasure even before then.

IT'S ALL ABOUT OBEDIENCE

I think our consecration is especially tested when we watch those closest to us suffer the consequences of our obedience, when our wives and children are called to carry *our* cross *with* us. Of course, being in the Philippines didn't just represent my obedience; but as the ordained head of my home, I knew that *I* was primarily responsible for our being there, and that I was *most* responsible for paying the price in prayer. I write this humbly, but I feel that it must be written: If attrition has never been higher among western missionaries, could it be because our prayer lives have never been lower? Our consecration to obedience must include childlike, fervent, and persistent prayer; or we may . . . we *will* end up taking back our sacrifice and robbing ourselves of untold blessing. "Watch and pray," Jesus said, "lest you enter into temptation. The spirit indeed is willing, but the flesh is weak" (Matthew 26:41).

Tim's patience and prayer cover gave me the space I needed to allow God to change my expectations – both of myself and my new appointment. I distinctly remember the day I said to God, "Dear Father, I will stay here until I'm old and dying if this is what you want and if you promise to be with me and enable me to do this task." I began practicing the admonition so often touted by one of the most inspirational women in my life, Elisabeth Elliot. She so often offered the most simple, yet profound, advice to, "Do the next thing." This became my mantra. If to "do the next thing" meant facing the fearsome tricycle ride into town to buy food, enduring an afternoon brownout in the blazing heat, lighting that blasted stove, or teaching my kindergartner how to read, I would just do it. Ever so slowly, as I embraced this attitude, God began to change me. I found a new underlying resilience that was not self-induced but divinely given in direct proportion to my willing obedience.

It didn't happen overnight, but God did graciously fill me with joy and passion for his work. By his grace I was able to lift up my eyes to the beautiful people he had surrounded us with and to *their* pain and suffering. He opened doors of ministry which far exceeded anything that we could have imagined. He allowed us to live and serve with the most amazing Filipino pastors and their wives – true heroes of the faith from whom we learned so much. He enabled us to offer the hope of redemption to those wounded and broken by sin.

There were times in the following years that I would reflect with shame upon that first year in the Philippines. My difficulties, complaining spirit, and lack of faith would come before me; and I was often tempted to allow Satan to overwhelm me with the painful memories.

One steamy night, I decided to get outside and enjoy a bit of exercise. Because it was rainy season, I was unable to walk the path around the campus and instead walked laps around the covered basketball court. As I walked, Satan began shouting out my past failures. The longer I walked the more he hammered me, until even the roar of the pounding rain on the tin roof seemed to harmonize in agreement with him. I listened with sadness. I felt deep remorse. Then I heard another voice – the still small voice of the Holy Spirit. His was a different voice – a voice of comfort, rather than condemnation. His words truly set me free. "Becky," he so lovingly whispered, "all those years ago I wasn't condemning you for how you *felt*, for your like or dislike of this place. I didn't expect perfection. What I asked of you was obedience, and you obeyed! This is what matters *most* to me."

I realized in a nanosecond that everything in one's life worthwhile to God *begins* with a heart of obedience. Success doesn't begin with our ability. Success doesn't depend on how we feel or don't feel. Success in the kingdom simply begins with the act of pure, sincere obedience. And the fruit of that obedience will be mouthwatering and sweet.

IT'S ALL ABOUT OBEDIENCE

There will be a day when joy will catch up with you. Joy will arise from the deepest part of your heart and carry you along this path of obedience. You will find, as we did, that life will be so much more than merely doing the next thing. I found that by first choosing to "Delight [myself] in the Lord" I was also discovering the true meaning of delight; and that the more I delighted, the more my desires were granted. Slowly, almost imperceptibly at first, my desires changed and became one with his. I realized that this was his plan from the very beginning – that my life would be full of meaningful, joy-filled service.

Where are you right now? Are you wallowing in disillusionment in the place where God has placed you? Are you struggling with thoughts like, *This is not the life I signed up for – the spouse I dreamed of, the perfect children I envisioned, the fulfillment I "deserve"?* Has your enthusiasm for obedience waned under the strain of the endless "nitty-gritty" of life? Does there seem to be no glory, pleasure, or gain in your sacrifice for God?

I urge you to walk on. Tim and I have often been challenged by a profound quote discovered in Lettie Cowman's *Streams in the Desert*. It simply states, "The glory of tomorrow is rooted in the drudgery of today." Let me simplify. Almost without exception, the glory of your marriage tomorrow is dependent on your respectful, loving actions today. The glory of your children's tomorrow will directly correspond to the prayer, attention, and care that you invest in them today. It is almost certain that the fruit you so long for in your ministry will multiply in direct proportion to your faithful planting, nurturing, and watering today. Perhaps the glory of a peaceful, organized home tomorrow is rooted in learning to manage your time today. The glory of earning that degree, finishing that project, losing that weight lies in the countless, sometimes difficult and inglorious choices that you make today.

Your obedience today will take you from a narrow and difficult life of duty and place you on the cusp of a delightful walk

of service. The success and blessings that God has in store for you tomorrow will never become a reality until you embrace the difficulty of today. Your life will never be without sacrifice and pain; but if you will not faint from weariness, joy will be measured out in proportion to the pain. Fulfillment will surpass failure, and the light of God's presence will ultimately dispel the darkness.

God's promise to the obedient is this: "But the path of the just is like the shining sun, that shines ever brighter unto the perfect day" (Proverbs 4:18).

CHAPTER FIVE

Faith and the Life of Obedience

*And he could there do no mighty work, save that he laid his
hands upon a few sick folk, and healed them.
And he marveled because of their unbelief.
And he went round about the villages teaching.*
Mark 6:5-6

Faith is the most critical component of an obedient and fruitful
life, but we will never experience it secondhand. Faith is established one answer to prayer and one personal encounter with God
at a time.

Great missionary to China, Hudson Taylor, refused to go to
war with untested weapons! In his autobiography, he tells how
he conditioned himself for missionary work years before he ever
set sail. (I should warn you that his methods will sound extreme
to most of us, myself included, but there is a crucial point to be
made.) At one point young Hudson removed his mattress so that
he could learn how to sleep on hard surfaces. Then, he imposed
upon himself the discipline of eating only brown bread and water
and learned that he was quite strong enough to walk up to eight
miles a day on this bland diet. The greatest test commenced, however, after he'd determined not to remind his godly, but sometimes
forgetful, employer about payday.

Hudson Taylor's employer, a medical doctor with many pressing demands, had requested that he be reminded at the end of each week when his faithful employee's salary was due. But Taylor, believing there would be countless moments in his missionary career when he would be in want and knowing that in those moments he would be completely dependent on God to touch the hearts of friends and family members back "home" regarding his needs, saw this as an opportunity to test the promises of God. He would keep quiet, he promised himself, and put faith to the test. And it was a test! Payday came and went without mention of the salary by the doctor. Days passed. Taylor was down to his last coins. Rent was due. Pressure was mounting. Then finally . . . the answer came! He testifies that this event was one of the most important of his life. But why? The answer, I think, is found in the following paragraph:

> I continued pleading with God, more and more earnestly, that he might graciously remind my employer that my salary was overdue. Of course, it was not want of money that distressed me – that could have been had at any time for the asking – but the question uppermost in my mind was this: "Can I go to China? Or *will my want of faith and power with God prove to be so serious an obstacle as to preclude my entering upon this much-prized service*?" (emphasis added).

Tim and I believe that a lack of faith precludes too many gifted men and women from "entering upon this much-prized service," whatever that service might be. If we don't learn to trust God for daily bread, for protection, for the emotional and spiritual needs of our families, and for the wisdom and strength for service, we're going to miss out on so many adventures. This is why it is so important to cultivate trust right now, right here!

Tim and I have both been left with a legacy of faith. This legacy, passed on to us by godly parents and grandparents, has shaped a trustful walk with God and sustained our obedience more than we can possibly express.

I can recall being awed as a child hearing my parents, James and Sue Keaton, give praise to God for his provision for our very large family. I was the sixth child born into a family of nine children. Although sharing life with such a "crowd" was quite normal for me, there seemed to be no end to people's curiosity about our family. I grew up being accustomed to being asked all sorts of questions. I remember one in particular that we were asked many times. "How long does a loaf of bread last at your house?" My dad always got a kick out of answering, "Well, I reach in with my left hand and grab the first heel; and by the time my right hand comes around, I grab the other heel!" There was more truth to that than one might think.

One evening after putting all nine of us to bed, Mom sent Dad to the store for only one item – well, actually, ten of one item. She needed ten loaves of bread to get her brood of hungry kids through the upcoming week. Dad set out on his mission, not telling Mom that he only had one dollar in his pocket. He was quite sure that this wouldn't be sufficient to purchase the needed amount of bread and actually talked to God about it on the short drive to the grocery store. Dad recounts that just as he walked into the store, he heard the manager announce over the loud speaker that they were having a sale on a cart full of bread and that for the next few minutes it would be a mere ten cents a loaf. Dad quickly made his way to that cart, picked up the ten loaves, paid for them, and walked out of that store with his heart bursting with praise. Although this may seem miniscule to some, Dad recalls being overwhelmed with the detailed love and care of his heavenly Father. He and Mom rejoiced and were careful to share this story with us, reminding us that those who obey and serve God can be sure of his provision.

Tim vividly recalls occasions in his boyhood days when God came through for their family in ways which can only be explained as divine intervention. **These stories were told and retold throughout his boyhood days, and they made a deep impression on his heart.** From his third year to his seventh year, for instance, Tim's father, Robert Keep, pioneered a small congregation in the beautiful hills of West Virginia. His salary was very small; and since he was working full-time to nurture the congregation and construct a chapel, the Keep family sometimes found themselves without food for their next meal. Credit cards were almost unheard of in the seventies. He recalls how over the course of those years God provided for their family in ways that he and his siblings will never forget. My husband continues:

> I well remember my mother, Grace, gathering my older sister, Janel, my younger brother, Dave, and myself around her and leading us in very specific prayers for food, clothes, shoes, Christmas gifts, and other practical needs. She often reminded us in those moments that since we'd *obeyed* God we could count on him caring for us. And, he did care for us.
>
> I'll never forget the neighbor lady who knocked on our door just minutes after one of those prayer meetings with Momma. She was a little frustrated because she had fixed a huge meal for her husband, Frank, but he had come home in a foul mood and refused to eat. She wondered if our family could eat a hot meal!
>
> And then there was the egg truck that broke down in front of our country home. The driver didn't want the eggs to spoil, so he wondered how many dozen we could use. He must have given us dozens of eggs, because I remember that we ate them prepared every way you can think of until we had had our fill of eggs! Sometime later another truck broke down nearby. This time it was a bread truck, and our family had more bread in our freezer than we could eat in weeks.
>
> I have clear memories of the old green Camaro which was donated to us by a farmer. When we went to pick it up, it was sitting in the middle of the pasture with weeds growing up through the floor. Some answer to prayer, right? But, it cleaned

up amazingly well, and we drove it for a couple of years until one afternoon a Coke truck rear-ended us while we slowed for a turn on a back country road.

I also remember the time that the Lord instantly healed my infected eyes after a godly lady (Sis. Grey) anointed me with oil, and how the Lord provided for our family when my father was hospitalized once for two weeks.

These stories and dozens more throughout my childhood formed within my heart a confidence in God, and through their trusting obedience my parents have made it much easier for my siblings and me to count on God in the tough spots of life.

Soon after Tim and I were married and moved to Hobe Sound, Florida to begin preparing for the ministry, we realized that we could not build our lives on these experiences alone. We began to realize that successful, sustained obedience demanded that we experience God's power in our own family.

I'll never forget the night God began to reveal himself to us as the God who hears and answers prayer. Tim was enrolled full time in Bible school and was working about 35 hours a week for a landscaping company. I was in nursing school at Indian River Community College. The program I was enrolled in was an accelerated program, and I was in class from 8:00 a.m. to 4:00 p.m. Monday through Friday. I spent nearly every spare moment studying, which limited my ability to work a regular job. I cared for an elderly gentleman on Saturday and Sunday mornings in an effort to earn some much-needed money for expenses. We were barely scraping by on our meager paychecks.

On this particular Sunday night, I shared with Tim that I had a $200 balance on my school bill that needed to be paid by the next morning. Our account was dismally short of that amount and, though we tried, neither of us could think of a solution. It had been a long day, and we turned in at around midnight feeling tired and discouraged. At Tim's suggestion, we stopped worrying for a few minutes and simply reminded God of our obedience, of his promises, and of our financial need. He was the only one who knew of our need, and he was the only one who could provide. Our prayer was short but sincere.

At 12:10 a.m., only minutes after our "Amen," we were startled by the sound of the doorbell. Tim jumped up and ran to the door wondering who in the world would be calling at this late hour. He was surprised to find a friend of ours standing there. She apologized for disturbing us, thrust an envelope in Tim's hand, and turned to go. As she walked away, she said over her shoulder that God had strongly impressed her and her husband to bring us this gift. Tim thanked her, and she was gone into the night. Moments later, he walked into our bedroom wearing a look of astonished delight on his face and holding a check for the amount of exactly $200. We laughed and thanked God for this unbelievable answer to prayer. It was our first time to experience such a specific answer to prayer as a married couple, though it certainly wouldn't be the last. This was the same reliable God – the one who had provided for our parents as they walked in obedience – now extending that same faithful provision to us as *we* walked in obedience.

One thing we learned in those early days of marriage is that faith is strengthened in us through *very specific* answers to prayer. Vague prayers get vague results and cannot strengthen faith; but when we petition God for specific requests, we give him a chance to answer specifically and thereby reveal his trustworthiness. My husband describes another moment in our preparation years when we "desperately" needed $50 ($50 might as well have been $5,000 in those days):

> After my classes one morning, I hurried home, changed into my work clothes, wolfed down a quick lunch, and prepared for my boss to pick me up to take me to our job site on Jupiter Island.
>
> All morning long I had struggled to concentrate on my classes for worry over a $50 doctor bill. I had no idea how we

were going to pay it. Both Becky and I were working as hard as we could, but with a new baby to care for (Valerie), tuition payments, and other household expenses, we just didn't have it.

While I was fretting inwardly over this need, it suddenly occurred to me that I should pray about it, that I should take this opportunity to cast this care upon the Lord and to ask him specifically for $50. I remember that I was alone in our little mobile home on Sunrise Way and that I became very fervent in my pleading with God. At last a most amazing peace settled over me. I got up knowing that the Lord was going to provide $50 somehow.

After about five minutes, I heard my boss drive up; but before I could grab my water jug and head out the door, he got out of his truck and knocked. I thought that was odd because every other day he'd just wait for me in the truck. When I opened the door, he thrust a piece of paper in my hand and simply said, "Tim, for some reason I just felt that I needed to give you this." With that he turned and headed back to the truck.

When I opened my hand, I noticed that the piece of paper was a check, and that the check was written for the amount of exactly $50. When I saw the amount in the box, I felt this incredible joy and sense of wonder arise in my heart. I laughed out loud! And I realized that my happiness was not because of the money but because I felt so *affirmed* and *cared for* by God. I was totally amazed by his rapid response to my prayer. I felt overwhelmed by his personal care for Becky and me. That day marked the dawning of a brighter day in my relationship with God.

Like almost everyone else, I've had personal struggles with feelings of insignificance and "ordinariness," but through encounters with God early in my Christian life – encounters such as this – I became increasingly aware of the value God placed on me. His love surprised me. His Fatherly heart drew me. This, and many other undeniable answers to specific prayers in those college days, witnessed to Becky and me that this God we'd committed our lives to is a living God – one who listens to us, walks with us, and makes our burdens his own.

IT'S ALL ABOUT OBEDIENCE

These initial answers to prayer early on in our journey as a couple were the foundation stones for a journey of obedience. Little did we know how vital these first stones would be.

Tim and I are sure that trusting the Lord for daily bread will progress to trusting him for "larger" things: training up children, the complex challenges of ministry, culture adjustments, and countless kingdom projects. As God's purposes for our families unfolds, our trust in his power will increase . . . little by little.

In 1997 our newborn son, Jesse, was discovered to have eye cancer.[1] During his four year battle with this disease, which resulted in blindness, I strongly believed that our returning to the Philippines would be contingent upon whether or not he retained his sight. I stated to Tim very confidently on several occasions that blindness would be the unmistakable "closing of the door." I mean, who takes a blind child to a third world country to live? Here in the United States there are seemingly endless resources for the physically disabled, but I just couldn't imagine how God could provide what Jesse needed in such an underdeveloped country.

When God clearly and unmistakably revealed to both Tim and me just two months after Jesse lost his sight that we should, indeed, return to the Philippines, I couldn't have been more surprised. Although I knew without a doubt that this was the path of obedience for us, that knowledge didn't necessarily remove every fear of the unknown.

Humanly speaking, this return made no sense. We had no idea how Jesse would be educated, how we would be able to afford the equipment needed for braille transcription, or who would *do* the braille transcription. We knew only two things. One, we were supposed to return. Two, the Lord would provide.

---

1. The story of how God carried our family through this crisis has been written about in my book entitled, *Eyes to See: Glimpses of God in the Dark.*

FAITH AND THE LIFE OF OBEDIENCE

Let me pause here to say that I'm *not* advocating reckless or irresponsible behavior. I am *not* saying that what the Lord "required" of us was "normal" for every Christian, for I realize God's plan for every life is unique. There is sometimes a temptation on the journey of faith of using God to validate our own desires. Had this been the case with us, I'm sure that our return to the Philippines would have been a dismal failure.

In the days leading up to our January 2002 departure for the Philippines, Tim and I sought answers to the most important questions. Before we boarded that plane, we did as much "homework" as we could and, through some great missionary friends, discovered Mylen. We learned that Mylen was a young Filipino teacher who had received training through a Christian organization in Manila called Resources for the Blind. "RFB" trained Filipinos in braille transcription and sent them out to villages all over the Philippines as tutors of blind students. These trained tutors taught hundreds of children and college age students to read and write braille, transcribed classroom materials, and so much more. Through our missionary friends, we learned that Mylen's assignment was with a group of blind college students just fifteen minutes from our home.

Mylen commuted from Manila to Pangasinan Province (our province) by bus each week and lived and worked Monday through Friday on the campus of the Wesleyan Bible College. When we inquired as to her willingness and availability to work with Jesse, she was very interested, but honest. She let us know that she had had no experience in working with blind children, only adults, but that if we would be patient with her she would be more than willing to try.

Mylen was a tiny little lady who walked with a cane due to having been stricken with polio as a little girl. She was amazing with Jesse and, after a bit of a rough start, they got along famously! I remember driving Jesse on Monday, Tuesday, and Thursday afternoons to spend an hour with her. I'd park our little SUV under a large Acacia tree and pray while he was inside. He behaved better if I stayed outside . . . and especially when I prayed!

Mylen began by teaching Jesse the braille alphabet, which he learned to write using a slate and stylus, as well as a large clunky contraption called a Perkins Braille Writer, a machine with the appearance of an old-fashioned typewriter but with only six keys. By using a combination of these six keys, one can create every letter and symbol in braille. The slate and stylus, as well as the Perkins brailler, works by pressing raised dots onto thick paper. This Perkins brailler cost around $700.00 and was kindly donated to our family by one of our supporting churches – yet another of God's many provisions. After each lesson on the Wesleyan campus, I'd go into the tiny sweltering room where "Ate Mye" ("Big sister Mye," as Jesse came to know her) and Jesse studied together to get an update on what he had learned and what his homework would be.

Jesse learned so quickly that I decided to learn right along with him! It was fun for me, and I loved feeling as if I was entering his world a bit by reading and writing braille. It also came in handy for reading his Christmas lists each year; and once when the "tooth fairy" forgot to do her job, she left a brailled note under his pillow apologizing for being late. He was impressed to say the least. During those early days, it was so exciting for us to watch his chubby four-year-old fingers slide over the tiny dots as he began reading words and then sentences.

After several months of working with Mye, our brand new English/Tagolag academy was ready to launch its very first school year. This was a vision that was finally being realized through the expertise and guidance of our coworkers, David and Christina Black. After much thought, prayer, and conversation with Christina, we made the decision to enroll Jesse in kindergarten. We made arrangements with Mylen and kept our schedule with her at least two afternoons a week. This was the beginning of my role as Jesse's braille transcriptionist. With fear and trembling, I tackled the job of transcribing his kindergarten worksheets. In the beginning it was easy. I'd simply have to braille upper and lower case letters which he could then match by drawing a line from one to the other. I would write above each series of dots so that his teacher could grade his work. This worked well, but it was certainly not without trial and error.

I read recently in one of my journals from those days that I had spent seven hours adapting Jesse's first math booklet into a format he could use. I did everything the hard way back then. Most of this little booklet was teaching simple number recognition. It would show, for example, a picture of three fish. Off to the right of the picture of fish would be three numbers that Jesse would have to choose from. It makes me smile now to think of how I glued tiny sequins on to each fish making them tactile. I then brailled the numbers onto thick sticky paper and attached the numbers over the print ones on the page. This was a forever process, and I knew it wouldn't be a sustainable one. Mye quickly showed me how to transcribe the same concept onto braille paper by brailling three cells to represent the fish and then the three numbers for him to choose from. This simplified my work considerably. I could braille an entire math booklet in barely an hour after learning this trick.

I recently watched a home video that I took of Jesse's first day of kindergarten. I was reminded of how God's grace works in our lives, enabling us to do what seems to be at times just downright ludicrous. **It was humorous, as well as a bit shocking, to watch this small blind boy weaving his way through a crowd of tiny Filipino kids, all of whom were staring at him curiously as he tapped along with his white cane.** Most notable, however, was that although everyone was talking, there was not a word of English being spoken. The kids were chattering loudly in Ilocano (the local dialect), and a teacher was giving instructions to the excited children in Tagalog (the national language). I had to wonder as I watched this video replay, *What was I thinking?* and more importantly, *What was going through Jesse's head on this first day of school?* Not only was he walking in the dark, but he couldn't understand a word that was being spoken. Humanly speaking, I know that I could never do this over again. It's only now that I'm beginning to see just how much grace God was pouring out in our lives. A part of this might be that I'm older and *softer* now, but I praise God for giving us the strength to do what was best for our son at that time.

Jesse *loved* his kindergarten teacher. He called her "Teacher Eva." She spoke both English and Tagalog in the classroom, and this enabled him to follow the lessons and to interact with the class. In the beginning, she was a bit terrified of teaching a blind boy and pandered to Jesse in less than helpful ways, as the following story illustrates. Jesse came home on the first day of school and informed me that he could not be tardy for class because Teacher Eva had explained to the class that they would have an apple removed from their behavior tree if they were late. This concerned him greatly *until* the day he was late and nothing happened. He figured out *very quickly* that the rules that applied to the *other* children weren't meant for *him*, because he was a *poor little blind boy*! This caused me no small amount of stress as getting this kid out the door on time in the mornings became almost impossible. I finally walked over to the academy and had a friendly chat with Teacher Eva. I told her that it really *was* okay for her to give our son consequences for bad behavior. Jesse was devastated when the next time he sauntered into class late he was instructed to remove an apple from his tree. Problem solved!

We found that the teachers at school did tend to hover over Jesse in an attempt to protect him. One day he came in from recess and said, **"Mom, Teacher Eva won't let me swing high! Mom, I can't *live* if I can't swing high!"** We enjoyed a good laugh from this expression of frustration; but I did try to explain to Jesse's teachers that he really was a normal kid, and that he could do almost anything other children his age could do. I encouraged Teacher Eva to come to me if she was unable to figure out a way for him to participate in an activity. Perhaps together we could figure out a way to make it possible. She was wonderful, and we will be forever grateful for her willingness to accept Jesse into her class. It was almost unheard of in the Philippines for a blind child to go to a regular school.

Jesse made many friends in school, but I'll never forget the day he ran into the house and exclaimed, "Mommy, you won't *believe* what happened to me today!" He went on to tell us that a sweet little female classmate had sneaked up on him and kissed him. He was horrified!

Another day while I was in town shopping, Jesse's artificial eye fell out and landed like a marble on his desk. He was embarrassed and quickly scooped it up, exited the classroom, and ran all the way home. Thankfully, I don't think his classmates even noticed what had happened. I received a panicked phone call from Valerie. She had no idea how to put the eye back in; and though I tried to talk her through the procedure over the phone, she managed to get it in upside down. Jesse was not amused, so I instructed Valerie to just patch his eye and send him back to school. I remember thinking that day, *My goodness, you can't make this stuff up!*

Between the academy and the faithful tutelage of Mylen, Jesse received eight years of superb education. When Jesse was in second grade, Mylen began coming to our home and staying three days every week. Jesse's workload at school was increasing, and I desperately needed help with the transcription process.

We learned of an amazing piece of equipment that would exponentially lighten the load of transcribing Jesse's work into braille. I was currently spending two to three hours a day pounding away on the Perkins brailler. It's a very "hard touch" machine, and I'd lie in bed at night with aching wrists and forearms from this repetitive work. We began to pray and ask God to supply the several thousand dollars that we would need to purchase the new equipment. We prayed in faith, but honestly felt as though we might have been asking for the moon!

It was almost unbelievable to both of us when we received an email from a pastor friend. He told us of the death of a long time church member, a dear elderly lady who had prayed for and supported our family for years. She especially had loved and prayed for Jesse during his four-year battle with cancer. He went on to tell us that she had left a considerable sum of money to our family, to be used for Jesse's needs. Our hearts were overwhelmed with the knowledge that there is nothing too difficult for the God we serve. We purchased a computer program which enabled us to transcribe Jesse's schoolwork using special software. We would then send the documents to the braille embosser for printing. I remember that we kept the embosser in the guest room with the door closed, as it made a dreadful racket while embossing the braille. It was much like having a jack-hammer pounding away in the next room! We were unspeakably grateful for this blessing, even with its noise, as this enabled Mylen to take over the transcription process for me.

It has been both thrilling and humbling for our family to experience God's gracious provision over and over again. Sometimes we've felt shame at the provisions we've squandered through unbelief. Sometimes the Holy Spirit has made us aware of moments we should have waited on him here or there or trusted him for this or that. But as a father pities his children, so the Lord has pitied us; and when we have confessed our failure, he has returned to bless us again.

It should go without saying that our family is nothing special. We wrote this chapter to say this: Every family can experience the power of God; every family can experience his favor. Jesus is "the same yesterday, today, and forever." But the power and the favor can only come through humble, obedient trust.

Every Christian family needs its very own faith narratives – unique and distinctive moments when God undeniably shows up! It will be difficult for our children to believe God – or even to believe *in* God – if they haven't witnessed God's unmistakable answers to prayer. Skeptics are often raised in Christian homes where there is much talk *about* God, but little or no encounters *with* God. May you and your family *know* that the gospel is not just words, but also power as you personally experience a living, loving God actively at work in both the minute and mountainous challenges of your life.

CHAPTER SIX

Wrestling with the Enemy

*Unless God has raised you up for this very thing, you will be
worn out by the opposition of men and devils. But if God
be for you, who can be against you? Are all of them
together stronger than God? O be not weary
of well doing!*
John Wesley, in a letter to William Wilberforce

*There are two equal and opposite errors into which our race
can fall about the devils. One is to disbelieve in their
existence. The other is to believe and to feel an
excessive and unhealthy interest in them. They themselves
are equally pleased by both errors and hail a materialist or a
magician with the same delight.*
C. S. Lewis

It was late in the evening when Tim and a small group of pastors climbed a steep mountain trail deep in the highlands of the Philippines. They had been summoned to pray for "a sick little girl." That was all the information they were given. But the moment they stepped over a low fence and into the yard, it felt as though they had stepped into hell. "My blood just froze," Tim says. "I felt that I was in the presence of evil. I had never experienced anything like this before." The pastors sensed this, too.

The young tribal girl was completely unresponsive. Her breathing was hoarse and very strange. She looked dead. "She's been like this for days," her family reported. Tim felt like he was living one of those dramatic scenes in the Gospels where a child was being tortured by an "unclean spirit." He describes what happened over the next thirty minutes:

> Pastor Yucaddi held the girl in his arms while we sang songs which magnified Christ's victory over sin and all the works of darkness. *"There is power . . . healing . . . victory in the name of Jesus,"* we sang. We also sang, *"There's power, power, wonder working power in the blood of the Lamb. . . ."* After we prayed over this beautiful girl, we carried her down the mountain and into the newly built church (the first in this remote mountain village). We laid her on the rough, wooden floor in front of the altar; and as more believers gathered around, we continued to sing and pray.
>
> After about 15 minutes, a most amazing peace filled the room. The little one became very still, as if sleeping. **Fifteen minutes more passed, and she suddenly opened her eyes, sat up, and asked for a drink of water.** She then stood up and walked out of the church as if she had never been sick. It was incredible! We rejoiced together in the power of God. The next morning, I saw the little girl running and playing with the other children.

One of the reasons I share this story is to remind us that, as Christians, we are in a very real spiritual battle; and we must be ready for it. Sadly, even ardent Christian workers have been wounded in spiritual battles they were ill-equipped to fight. Many more gifted, yet spiritually untrained or undisciplined recruits, have been turned back by an enemy far more powerful than they had anticipated. Many today have wandered from the path of obedience simply because they were unprepared for the intense opposition they would face, or perhaps they were skeptical of such things. **The enemy may not come against you as *overtly* as experienced in the above story, but he *will* come against you**. Obedience will not go uncontested. The casualty rate is alarming. Spiritual warfare is real.

> *Finally, my brethren, be strong in the Lord and the power of his might. Put on the whole armor of God that you may be able to stand against the wiles of the Devil. For we do not wrestle against flesh and blood, but against principalities, against powers, against the rulers of the darkness of this age, against spiritual hosts of wickedness in the heavenly places. Therefore take up the whole armor of God, that you may be able to withstand in the evil day, and having done all, to stand* (Ephesians 6:10-12).

Before moving to the Philippines, I had heard hair-raising stories of spiritual warfare told by missionaries; and, honestly, these had always frightened me. Overt spiritual warfare was not something that I had previously encountered. While I had been mostly protected from this reality my whole life, Tim and I found that in the third world the spirit world is sometimes much more visible and tangible. The absence of spiritual light offers the powers of darkness the cover they need to do their grossest evils. Many believe that having been left unchallenged for centuries – in many nations – demonic powers have been able to establish territorial strongholds. Though the spirit world holds many mysteries, it does seem that with no faith-filled prayer to resist them and no word – no gospel – to expose them, evil spirits hold generations of "gospel-less" pagans hostage. And they thrive on ignorance and superstitious fear. Perhaps this is why they so often hover frighteningly close to the surface of daily life. In America, we tend to either ignore the reality of spiritual warfare or develop an unhealthy preoccupation with it. Either extreme is a dangerous deception. Extremes have cultivated indifference or cynicism toward the spirit world, and cynicism has left many Christian workers vulnerable to attacks.

I want to emphasize that to walk with Jesus on the path of obedience is a secure place, a place where we can stand firm, and it is a place of sweet comfort and fellowship. However, it is also a place of increased danger, and intensified spiritual battles are realities many missionaries will identify with. The following excerpt is from a letter written by a missionary Tim has had the privilege of mentoring. It was written just a few months after he and his wife had arrived on the field.

> In addition to the culture shock, I think one of the huge challenges that I have faced is in the arena of spiritual warfare – not the kind of scary, overt demonic attacks like I've heard missionaries speak about – but intense seasons of temptation, both subtle and not-so-subtle. At times, it seemed like a relentless bombardment from the enemy. I'm thankful to report that by the grace of God I have been victorious. I can see now why you warned me (early on) to prepare for spiritual conflict. I have found the Word of God and the shield of faith to be a great source of strength and refuge during this time.

Spiritual watchfulness is so important. Had Tim and I not become *aware* of the *much-increased* spiritual warfare early on in our cross-cultural experience, I'm sure we would not have survived very long. Had we not *graciously* been made aware of some of the strategies of Satan, we would not have withstood his onslaughts. Let me just briefly outline some of Satan's strategies as Tim and I experienced them:

- A sense of oppression and discouragement out of our "normal" range

- Overt demonic attacks

- Covert attacks, such as physical sicknesses which seemed to involve a spiritual element, a rise in temptation's temperature, abnormal marital conflict, or conflict with coworkers and nationals and intense irritability and sensitivity

Here are a few of our stories.

We were stunned and devastated when toward the end of our first year of ministry in the Philippines our newborn son Jesse was diagnosed with a very aggressive cancer in the eyes. *Was there a "spiritual" element to this? Was Satan trying to throw us off course, to hinder the work God wanted to do through us?* We didn't really give this much thought until we received a letter from a wise veteran missionary and mentor, Dr. Paul Turner, who gently admonished us to not allow Satan to steal the spiritual momentum God had granted us. Without being sensational or dramatic, he simply reminded us that there was more than merely a physical aspect to our son's diagnosis. We never forgot this counsel. After four years of treatment and finally a cure, we returned as a family to the Philippines. Our children were a bit older. Valerie was now nine; Timothy Jr., seven; and newly-blind Jesse, four. **We arrived back in the Philippines with some fresh battle scars, but also with hearts strengthened and with a much deeper and more solid confidence in the love and power of God.** What Satan had intended for evil, God intended for good! This confidence would serve us well in the years to come.

We returned to the Philippines early in 2002 and hit the ground running. Tim was busy overseeing projects and new ministry developments within our mission work, teaching in the Shepherd's College, and developing leadership training for our pastors. New congregations were being planted, new missionaries had arrived, and new ministries were forming. It was a season of tremendous blessing.

I almost immediately had a steady stream of "patients" who would show up on our doorstep needing medical treatment. I loved this interaction with people! I began going to a nearby village on Sunday afternoons to share a Bible study with the women there. One thing led to another, and I began visiting this place regularly to help with specific health issues as they were presented. This village was a spiritually dark place. As I shared the gospel with these dear people each week and practiced my medical skills among them in order to in some small way alleviate some of their suffering, I began to understand just how hopeless life without Jesus really is. I witnessed the depths of depravity and superstition like I had never experienced. It was shocking and disturbing.

During this season of blessing I was awakened from a sound sleep in the dead of night. I hadn't dreamed or heard anything, but was seized with a grip of fear so strong I could scarcely breathe! I had no idea what I was afraid of. My heart was racing, and the very air that I breathed was thick with palpable terror. I had never experienced anything remotely similar to what I felt on that night. When I found my voice, I whispered "Tim." I was shocked when he answered me immediately, "Do you feel that?" He, too, was wide awake and had been lying there for some minutes paralyzed with the same heavy fear. We were both startled when our son Timothy, then seven, stumbled into our room. "Mom, Dad," he whispered, "I'm so afraid. It feels like something is choking me!"

It took us only a moment to realize that we were not wrestling against "flesh and blood," but against the "rulers of the darkness." With this awareness, Tim sat Timothy on the floor and simply opened the Bible to Psalm 91 and began to read. As he read, every word was alive with power and seemed to have been written just for us.

He who dwells in the secret place of the Most High shall abide under the shadow of the Almighty.

I will say of the Lord, "He is my refuge and my fortress; my God, in him I will trust."

WRESTLING WITH THE ENEMY

Surely he shall deliver you from the snare of the fowler and from the perilous pestilence.

He shall cover you with his feathers, and under his wings you shall take refuge; his truth shall be your shield and buckler.

You shall not be afraid of the terror by night, nor of the arrow that flies by day,

Nor of the pestilence that walks in darkness, nor of the destruction that lays waste at noonday.

A thousand may fall at your side, and ten thousand at your right hand; but it shall not come near you.

Only with your eyes shall you look, and see the reward of the wicked.

Because you have made the Lord, who is my refuge, even the Most High, your dwelling place,

No evil shall befall you, nor shall any plague come near your dwelling;

For he shall give his angels charge over you, to keep you in all your ways.

In their hands they shall bear you up, lest you dash your foot against a stone.

You shall tread upon the lion and the cobra, the young lion and the serpent you shall trample underfoot.

"Because he has set his love upon me, therefore I will deliver him; I will set him on high, because he has known my name.

He shall call upon me, and I will answer him; I will be with him in trouble; I will deliver him and honor him.

With long life I will satisfy him, and show him my salvation."

As these beautiful words were read in faith, each one was a flaming arrow against the dark presence in our room. Evil fled. Fear lifted. And peace flooded in dramatically. Tim read through tears. And by the end of the Psalm, Timothy was fast asleep. Our enemy could not stand in the presence of truth!

That night Tim and I were made vividly aware that we were advancing into enemy territory and that the enemy of God was not going to go without a fight. We believed that this was a direct counter attack. We were sobered by this awareness, but were equally infused with strength realizing that *"greater is he that is in you, than he that is in the world,"* and that the double-edged sword of truth was a weapon to be reckoned with. The comfort that flooded our hearts filled us with courage to continue in the battle. We knew with certainty that we could always expect God to "show up" and fight with us and for us.

God's power against the Enemy is vividly seen when he turns *even* our mistakes into a means of redemption, as the following story illustrates.

One morning, Tim and I headed out to do a little food shopping. We stopped by our local vegetable market to pick up some of the succulent fresh produce. After purchasing the needed fruits and vegetables, we returned to our vehicle. As we were leaving the marketplace, I suddenly realized that I had forgotten one item on my list. Tim pulled the van to the side of the road and prepared to run and get the forgotten item.

Tim opened the van door without seeing the small, severely stooped elderly woman walking by. The opening van door bumped her, sending her sprawling onto the pavement. She immediately began shrieking with pain. I jumped out of the van and ran around to see what had happened. I was filled with consternation at the sight of this tiny, frail lady lying there on the ground. It appeared that she was not only suffering great pain, but was also in shock. **Tim carefully picked her up and laid her in the back seat of our van.** She was all alone and spoke no English. A lady who was selling vegetables nearby saw Tim place her in the van. She came running over to us and explained that she knew this woman and her family. She offered to accompany us. We were greatly relieved, and the four of us set out for the nearest hospital.

When we arrived at a small clinic, they placed her in a wheelchair and left her waiting with us in the lobby. After only a few minutes, she started turning gray and passed out! They quickly got her into a bed; and, I must admit, we were nearly frantic with worry for this poor lady. Tim was painfully aware that this whole incident was his fault! Her family had not yet arrived, so we sat with her feeling helpless and very responsible!

It was a couple of hours later that her daughter came into the room breathless and nervous. I was sure that she was wondering what in the world these Americanos had done to her mother. We truly did not know what to expect from this family. *Would they be angry, seek vindication, sue us?* They were kind and understanding and, later that day, Tim transported them to a larger hospital where it was confirmed that this elderly lady, whose name we learned was Christina, did indeed have a fractured hip which would require surgery. It goes without saying that we felt absolutely horrible about this. After all, we were here to be a blessing and help people, not break the hips of little old ladies.

Tim and I supported this family through a most difficult surgery, and God provided a way for us to pay for Christina's total hip replacement. We were so thankful when she made a wonderful recovery. We developed a warm and lasting relationship with her entire family, and they opened their small barrio for us to come and begin Bible studies on Sunday afternoons. I went regularly to check on Christina's recovery and also treated her husband's varied health issues. The family began attending church each Sunday, and eventually both Christina and her husband received the Lord Jesus Christ. They became trophies of God's providential, redemptive grace. Today Christina is in heaven!

God gave us a new beautiful baby girl in July of 2003. We named her Carolyn Grace, after both grandmothers. At the tender age of seven weeks, she inexplicably stopped breathing. We were in church when this happened and immediately called for prayer. Several pastors prayed over her. After about a minute, she began breathing but immediately spiked a high fever and became very lethargic. We rushed her to Manila where a myriad of tests were run, but we received no definitive answers. We were mystified.

Dr. Vicky Ang, our pediatrician, sat us down to talk with us. We hadn't known her for very long, but knew that she was a vibrant Christian. We learned later that she had been raised a Buddhist, but had heard the gospel during medical school and had been wonderfully saved. She was the president of the Christian Doctors Association and had led many fellow physicians to the Lord. As we sat in her office that day, **she stated frankly that she had experienced this exact situation with more than one other missionary family**. She told us that she firmly believed that this was an attack of Satan against our family – a direct attack to discourage us from continuing with our calling. She explained this with the same confidence with which she may have given us lab results or an EEG reading. Tim and I were taken back by her words. At the time I'm not sure we were convinced, but left feeling grateful that our baby was okay.

In early January of 2004, I became very ill with the measles and was hospitalized for several days at St. Luke Hospital in Manila. I was finally discharged but remained terribly weak. We arrived home to find our five-month-old Carrie very sick, running a high fever and not sleeping or eating. It was apparent by the rash covering her body that she had also contracted the measles. She cried incessantly and refused to take any fluids. Our thirteen-year-old daughter, Valerie, with the help of our coworkers, David and Christina Black, had been caring for her. We learned that she had been in this condition for two days. Words cannot describe how completely exhausted and now frightened we felt. The spiritual oppression we felt at this time was some of the heaviest we had endured. When I saw how sick Carrie was, I begged Tim to take her to the hospital in Manila. I felt sure that she had the measles and knew how dangerous this could be for her. I'll let Tim describe the rest:

> I was so tired from the events of the week – sitting up beside Becky's hospital bed for days, caring for her and getting very little rest. I simply could not move another step. Becky was still very ill and could not make the trip back to the hospital. As I wrestled with what to do, the still voice of God spoke clearly to my heart. The thought came to me that we should do what James instructs us to do: to call for the elders of the church to pray for healing. I sent for Rev. Lauro Forto, our Shepherd's College administrator, Rev. Villamor Comilang, our campus pastor, and David Black. They came, and I asked them to pray for Carrie. As we prayed, the peace of God entered our living room and gave us strong assurance of healing.
>
> Instead of improving, however, Carrie seemed to worsen. Her screams became even higher pitched, and her little body burned with fever. Becky was nearing despair and again strongly suggested that we pack up and make the four hour trip back to Manila. Now, I am not sensational or inclined to foolishly risk the life of my child, but on this occasion I knew in my heart what God had spoken. I believed that this was a test. I placed Carrie in the bed between Becky and me and simply said aloud, "Father, we have prayed as you have instructed us to do; we are

in this moment claiming the victory that you have confirmed in our hearts; we are standing steadfastly on your Word."

Within five minutes, Carrie had not only stopped crying, but began nursing and soon fell asleep. From that moment, her condition improved; and she recovered completely. Praise the Lord!

When Carrie was seventeen months old, she came down with what appeared to be the stomach flu. It began with severe vomiting and diarrhea. A fever ensued which hovered around 104 degrees and stubbornly refused to come down. I was concerned but kept waiting for this fever to break. After all, the doctor's office was a four hour drive, and I felt confident that she'd recover without any medical intervention. I was giving all the nursing care that I knew to give, but her condition worsened.

I was embarrassed and alarmed when on the fourth day, Rev. David Yuccaddi stopped by the house. He took one look at Carolyn and took Tim aside. "You need to take your baby to the hospital," he said. This confirmed what my heart had been telling me, and I immediately chided myself for not making this decision earlier. We arranged for someone to look after our three older children and started driving to Manila.

By the next afternoon, as Carolyn's condition worsened, she was placed in the pediatric ICU. Tim and I watched her deteriorate with each passing moment. We had not been given a diagnosis, just told that she'd be given supportive care there until her body fought off whatever was ailing her. It was a strange and scary place: one big room with curtains surrounding each bed. I heard monitors beeping just beyond the thin curtain next to Carolyn's bed and curiously peered around it to see who was there. I was shocked to see a small boy, nine or ten years of age. He was on life support and emaciated. I couldn't help myself; I had to ask the nurse what his condition was. She explained that he was dying from complications from the measles. It shattered me to think that something so preventable was taking the life of this precious little boy.

My attention turned back to my own baby, and my worry was heightened. *What's wrong with her? And why is she not improving?* I wondered. I locked eyes with Tim who was standing on the other side of her bed. He gazed back at me and whispered, "What if she dies?" He wasn't trying to be dramatic; he was just stating what seemed to be a very real possibility. I couldn't' believe we were here. I mean, hadn't we just endured four years of cancer treatment? We had been to the brink of despair and back. I felt I couldn't face this kind of thing again. I began to cry and in my fragile state of mind said to him, "Honey, if and when she gets better, I am going home. I can't endure these kinds of situations anymore."

We stood there feeling lost and alone. We longed for our family, a pastor, a familiar face from home. Tim began to pray. He prayed for both of us. He reminded God that we were here in obedience to his call, our baby was so very sick, that we had no answers, no idea what her sickness was, or if she would recover. He then asked God to please send someone – anyone – who could help us, could help Carolyn.

Moments after his whispered "Amen," a tall Filipino doctor walked into the room. After introducing himself to us and telling us that he'd be looking after our baby, he moved to the bedside of our sick baby girl and began his exam. He worked confidently and thoroughly. He explained that he was fairly certain that she was suffering from a rare, but deadly, tropical virus. He went on to say that in the previous week he had "lost" two children to this virus. They had both been from our province. He said that in both cases the child had been brought to the hospital on the fifth day of their illness. We had brought Carolyn on the fourth day.

Tim and I were scared, but calm, as this doctor outlined a plan of treatment. The nurse in me questioned some of the seemingly ications he ordered to be administered, but he assured me that he knew what he was doing. He went on to tell me that he had served a six year fellowship in the pediatric ICU at Children's Hospital of Detroit, Michigan. I gaped at him. We had spent four years practically living at Children's Hospital of Michigan, as this is where Jesse had received all of his cancer treatment. Tim and I knew in that moment that God had indeed sent "someone" in the person of this doctor to help us, to help Carolyn. And help us he did! This kind man, whom we had never met, stayed by Carolyn's bedside all night long, even missing his grandmother's wake! With his expert care and watchful eye, she did recover; and we took her home a few days later.

Looking back on those dark days spent with Carolyn in ICU, I marvel at the good that God brought from them. It was during those long hours of waiting that we developed a deeper friendship with "Doctora" Vicky Ang. We learned that she is a passionate Christian who loves her country and people. We heard her heart of compassion for the lost and suffering. We talked about the little boy in the next bed and of the very simple vaccination that could have saved his life. And we began to talk and dream of working together to take desperately needed medical care deep into the mountains. She told me that if I would organize it, she would help. She promised to put together a team of doctors from St. Luke's Hospital to join us.

She kept her promise. Over the next few years, we joined hands and hearts and were able to treat thousands of sick Filipinos in remote places. We prayed with hundreds and witnessed many of these come to faith in Jesus Christ. I remember one specific day during one of those missions when I sat and watched Dr. Ang lovingly care for a nine-year-old boy. I listened as he poured his heart out to her. She told me later that he confessed that he had been lying to his parents and felt such guilt. She leaned close, looked into his eyes with such tenderness, and then shared the gospel with him. Under a tent in that remote village, he bowed his head and received the forgiveness Jesus offered. It was beautiful! It was incredible to see God take what Satan meant for evil and turn it into eternal good. **The sickness and near death of our little girl actually opened doors and blossomed into something so much bigger than ourselves**. "Greater is he that is in [us] than he that is in the world."

In my mind's eye, I can see Satan running in defeat with each redemptive act that took place as a result of his botched plan. With each immunization given, every wound lovingly cleaned, every grace-filled embrace, and every prayer prayed for the lost and lonely, he had to bow his head and turn away. I understand so well that there is truly *"no wisdom, no insight, no plan that can succeed against the Lord"* (Proverbs 21:30). God has a divine way of fulfilling his purposes in the world in spite of, and often in greater measure *because of,* the attempts of the enemy to defeat and discourage us.

You can be sure that walking the path of obedient service to God will gain the attention of our enemy. We must not underestimate him. I have found him to be a fearsome foe. But I've also thought of the young boy who faces the bully on the playground, one much bigger and stronger than he. He faces him, not because he thinks for one moment that he can conquer him, but because he knows that standing with him is his older, stronger, and loving brother.

We also have someone: the God of heaven and earth, always near and ready to deliver us. When we choose to tenaciously embrace the promises of God in the face of onslaughts, Satan is compelled to flee.

Has your experience with this "wrestling with the enemy" caused you to waver in your pursuit of God? Perhaps just anticipating what "engaging the enemy" may cost you has left you reticent in your obedience. Does taking the road of least resistance tug at your humanity? Do you fear what Satan can do to you more than you fear the Lord? Obedience is the essence of what it means to "fear the Lord." I challenge you to embrace it. Whatever that may mean for you, stand with unwavering resolve. You will find, dear friend, that you aren't standing alone, but that standing with you is God Almighty. Ray Comfort once said, "A blind, anemic, weak-kneed flea on crutches would have a greater chance of defeating a herd of a thousand wild, stampeding elephants than the enemy has of defeating God."

Each unique battle you will engage in will be won by these simple principles:

First, recognize the enemy. Seek wisdom to discern his strategy.

Second, always make prayer a priority.

Third, endeavor to be honest regarding your weaknesses. Confess failure.

Fourth, cultivate faith through constant meditation on the Word of God.

As you commit yourself to this road of obedience, you can rest assured that God is committing himself to you. With each battle and subsequent victory, you will know with certainty that *"the weapons we fight with are not the weapons of the world. On the contrary, they have divine power to demolish strongholds"* (2 Corinthians 10:4 NIV). Victory belongs to the Lord!

CHAPTER SEVEN

Nothing without Love

*If I speak with human eloquence and angelic ecstasy but don't
love, I'm nothing but the creaking of a rusty gate.
If I speak God's Word with power, revealing all his mysteries
and making everything plain as day, and if I have faith that
says to a mountain, "Jump," and it jumps,
but I don't love, I'm nothing.*
(1 Corinthians 13:1-2 The Message)

On an early afternoon in November, I stepped from my kitchen through a screen door, out onto my back porch, and discovered her sitting there. She was dirty, pregnant, and carrying a malnourished looking little boy on her hip. It took me a moment to recover from the shock of finding a complete stranger on my mostly-enclosed porch, but I quickly mustered a smile and asked, "Can I help you?" **In an expressionless tone, she told me that they were hungry**. I left them there and went inside to prepare a bit of something for the two of them to eat. Returning to the porch, I handed her a sandwich and some Ramen noodles and stood watching in astonishment at the manner in which her little boy devoured it. Without a doubt, this little guy was starving! Thus began my relationship with Jasmine and Mark.

They came often, appearing seemingly out of nowhere and simply asking for food, laundry soap, shoes, or some other necessity. Although I tried repeatedly to find out where Jasmine was from, she was evasive and never came or went through the gate, but always through the rice field behind our house. We often watched until the two of them disappeared into the adjacent mango grove.

Jasmine never smiled, said "thank you," or initiated conversation. Her son was silent, non-playful, and showed no expression when I attempted to interact with him.

Jasmine's eyes captivated me. They were large, round, and emotionally vacant. One day, as she prepared to leave, I gently laid my hand on her shoulder to pray for her. The moment I touched her, she flinched; and I saw the first flicker of emotion in those eyes. I saw fear and extreme discomfort.

By December, Jasmine and Mark were showing up every day. Mark began to smile as soon as we'd open the door, and Jasmine began to share bits and pieces of her life. I learned that her mother was a "hostess" who entertained men. Perhaps because she didn't know who her father was, she chose to tell us that he was a "rich" American, one of her mother's customers. I learned that she was often beaten by her husband who was an alcoholic and gambler.

Jasmine always came at the most inopportune times. Six o'clock in the morning was her favorite time to show up. Her knock on the door could raise the sleeping dead! It was loud and repeated until, fearing that she would awaken our own small children, we'd sleepily throw on some clothes and answer. Honestly, I became irritated with her continual forays into our privacy and even our sleep. She smelled awful! She had a scaly rash that covered her arms, and I had observed bugs crawling in her hair. I cringed at the thought of getting too close, fearing that I might contract a fungus, head lice, or something worse. *Really ... what is my responsibility here?* I often wondered. *Must we continue this indefinitely? There must be a limit somewhere!*

NOTHING WITHOUT LOVE

Over and over in my mind, I mulled many justifiable reasons for turning Jasmine and Mark away; but Tim and I both felt compelled by the Holy Spirit to continue meeting their needs. We knew that no matter what time of day or night she chose to come, we were to continue giving without restraint. **A question that always tugged at my mind was this:** *How does Jesus view Jasmine?* As I pondered the answer, I became aware of my lack of love – not only for her, but for the "unwanted" in this world. I began to pray and ask God to enable me to love this needy woman and child as he loved them.

Christmas came and went. Jasmine continued to come daily, and often twice a day. As her abdomen steadily grew, I knew that her delivery must be nearing. I bought clothes, diapers, blankets, and baby soap for the anticipated little one. She mentioned one day in early February that she wanted to have a girl. She went on to say that she had had a girl once, but that she had died on October 7 after a five-day illness. (I later verified this to be the truth.) I recalled the horrific condition that Jasmine had been in on the day of our first meeting in early November and soberly realized that she had buried her child only a few weeks previously.

One day shortly after this conversation, Jasmine abruptly stopped coming. I knew that she must have given birth. As I had yet to find out where she lived, I began inquiring in earnest around our little village. It wasn't long before I located the place.

On a Friday afternoon, a Filipino friend and I walked the short distance to her home. I was shocked as we walked past the main house on the property and under some trees to find her lying on the cement floor of a . . . piggery! It was a tiny eight by eight former pig stall! She lay there with Mark on one side of her and a tiny baby boy on the other. I learned from the neighbor that her house had been destroyed by a typhoon and that he had consented to let them clean out the piggery and move in.

Later that week, we visited with a team of American doctors and nurses. They examined the baby and gave needed vitamins, medicines, and a good supply of food to Jasmine and her children.

Although I had invited Jasmine to come to church on several occasions, she had always declined, saying, "I'm Catholic." Two weeks after the birth of her baby, she appeared again on my back porch. This time, she not only asked for food but for a dress to wear to church. I was surprised and asked her, "Do you want to come to church with me?" "Yes," she replied, "this Sunday."

Jasmine did come to church that Sunday and every Sunday after. I felt so blessed to have her walk to the front of the church with me. She listened with rapt attention as the sermon was delivered. Her visits to my house decreased to maybe once or twice each week. She'd come to remind me to pick her up for church.

It was only after a few Sundays that God's presence came very near as we were singing a beautiful praise chorus that says,

At the cross I bow my knee
Where your blood was shed for me
There's no greater love than this.[1]

I glanced at Jasmine and saw tears streaming from her eyes. The knowledge that she was loved seemed to be washing away the fear and distrust by which she had been bound for so long! *Lord, let it wash away her sins*, I prayed! **I placed my arm around her and realized that this cold-hearted "beggar," who had perhaps never felt a loving touch, heard a kind word, or experienced a compassionate deed, but had endured countless beatings and sexual abuse, was being melted by love.** I understood in a moment why we had been constrained for the past five months to patiently give, give, and give, even when our selfish hearts had wanted to send her away.

---

1. At the Cross, Hillsong

NOTHING WITHOUT LOVE

We will never accomplish God's purposes in this world until we learn to love as he loves; until we push past our own boundaries, frustrations, discomforts, and irritations and love as we have been loved – in the rags of our sin and brokenness. Think of the love Christ has demonstrated toward us. It's incomprehensible to think how far he condescended – down, down, down to our pitiful, sinful state. And his love continues to transcend race, class, mental ability, and so many other stipulations that we so often apply to our love.

Through Jasmine, I realized that just as she was dirty, smelly, unkempt, ungrateful, and even barbaric, this is exactly how we must appear to a holy and righteous God. And yet, he loves us! His love breaks through all of our filthiness, failures, unworthiness, and sin and draws us to himself.

It was a few weeks later that my friend Melcha and I met with Jasmine in our little bamboo square hut outside our home on a Sunday afternoon. We shared the simple gospel with her. With tears dripping from her face, she began recounting some of her sins. It was obvious as she spoke that she felt deep remorse. She had difficulty believing that God would indeed not only forgive, but forget, her shameful past. I shared with her that God promises to "hurl all our iniquities into the depths of the sea" (Micah 7:19 NIV). I assured her that God does forgive and that he does not hold our sins against us. Jasmine bowed her head that day and received the forgiveness of the Lord Jesus.

Our love did not solve all of Jasmine's problems. Her circumstances in life did not radically change. She continues to live in poverty. But love became a bridge which connected her to Jesus. He is the one who will walk with her, hold her, sustain her on life's bleakest days and envelop her in his everlasting arms. Then, at last – heaven! How wonderful that will be!

Without love our most noble sacrifices will come to nothing. Not long after Amy Carmichael arrived in India as a missionary, she met an old Indian man who said, "We've heard much preaching. Can you show us the life of the Lord Jesus?" Amy did. She didn't just talk love and compassion, but showed India and the world the life of the Lord Jesus by rescuing thousands of Indian girls from temple sex slavery and leading many of them to him in over fifty years of missionary service without a furlough.

Though neither Tim nor I realized it then, we went to the Philippines with a bit of a "we're here to straighten things out" mindset. We had been warned by good mentors of the sensational, superstitious tendencies of our Filipino congregations, as well as some "Christian disciplines they need to be taught." Many of these concerns were valid. While we missions leaders often mean well, however, we must be aware of the damage so often done in cross-cultural ministry when change is leveraged with law rather than love; when change is manipulated with money or education or . . . anything. This understanding didn't come easy for Tim, as the following story illustrates:

> Town fiestas in the Philippines provide days of pagan revelry –
> including a Gay Beauty Contest. In an attempt to reach out to
> evangelical Christians, our town mayor offered one night of the
> fiesta as Evangelical Night. On Evangelical Night, all evangelical
> churches would gather at the town square for a joint worship
> service with the hope that many of the towns unchurched would
> hear the gospel.
>
> Our first experience with Evangelical Night didn't go so
> well for me, but the lesson I would learn would position my
> heart for a more humble, Christ-like ministry.
>
> Hundreds of believers from various denominations were
> present in the open square that night. Our Shepherd's College
> faculty and student body were also present, as well as several
> pastors and congregations within our denomination. As a sign
> of respect to the "Americanos" present, our family was given VIP
> seating on the stage . . . right in front of two gigantic speakers!

NOTHING WITHOUT LOVE

When the band got revved up, the music became so loud that I felt my ears would explode! The music was not only loud, but the "worship" was too long; and I felt the songs most distasteful. To make matters dreadfully irreverent (from my perspective), one of the charismatic churches "blessed us" with young females who came to the front and performed a worship dance. It was more than my solemn, conservative sensitivities could handle. I was angry! I whispered sternly to Becky to grab the children because we were leaving this . . . irreverent place! So, we got up right in the middle of the service, jumped in our van, and headed back toward the campus – a brief three-kilometer drive.

On the way, I ranted a bit; but Becky was unusually quiet. I knew that I had embarrassed her. I knew, too, that her silence was a protest against my attitude. Three kilometers was all the distance the Holy Spirit needed to teach me one of the most powerful lessons I have ever learned. "Son," he said in my heart, "you acted tonight in self-righteous pride! I didn't call you here to change everything and everyone, to impose your personal standards and agenda, or even to force *my* principles and standards. I called you, first, to love people, through me, and to sincerely care for them. If you don't love them, you'll never be able to help them." This simple, convicting message from the Lord humbled me greatly; and I promised the Lord that, by his grace, I would throw away my agenda and let him use me where he saw fit. I realized that night that love would be our capital for transformation. In the days to come, I would also become increasingly aware of how much cultural differences, worldview, and life experiences play a big role in how we think and what we deem acceptable or unacceptable. In the years to come, I would have to work through what was biblical and theological and what was a matter of taste and preference.

Tim and I had to realize that without love we're just making noise. Love is more important than right answers. Love will not water down the truth, but love provides the capital we'll need to bring about needed change.

IT'S ALL ABOUT OBEDIENCE

One of our most thriving ministries today in the Philippines is a church planting work among the tribes of the Cordillera's of northern Luzon. Over the years we have thrilled to see the gospel changing lives – even "gambling queens," drunkards, and pagan priests. We've witnessed imprisoned souls set free, homes restored, and young people called into the harvest. Through faith, a tribal pastor's training center has been established, and many churches have been planted. Only a small handful of people know just how close we came to losing this ministry due to a lack of compassion and sensitivity to the Holy Spirit.

One day, the national visionary of this movement, Rev. David Yucaddi, came to my husband with a deep concern in his own family. Tim's advice, while "right" perhaps, was terse, harsh, heavy-handed, and so discouraged this man of God that he decided he must resign. As Tim learned of this and of the pain he had caused this pastor, the Holy Spirit awakened him to his need for a baptism of love – not only as a missionary but as a husband and father. In brokenness he wept before the Lord and this brother (who did not resign) and said that he felt such cleansing of the Holy Spirit that he knew he would never be the same! This amazing turning point in Tim's life and ministry reminds us that apart from love all our words, works, and sacrifices will amount to nothing.

Last year, Tim reminded a student body preparing for a life of ministry of Jesus' call to "hate your life in this world."

> You young people have been trained in this wonderful institution by some of the most gifted servants. You have been saturated with excellence: surrounded by majestic music, skilled communicators, and beautiful facilities. You've lived in a kind of stained-glass Christian atmosphere; interacted daily with exceptionally intelligent people; and enjoyed uplifting, tasteful worship.
>
> **Beware! These privileges and blessings make "hating your life in this world," for Jesus' sake, more difficult**. You

must develop the mind of Christ – the mind of a servant. You must be able to hold loosely to ideals and love people right where they are. You must wrap your arms around dirty, smelly people. You must be patient with "bad" theology, suffer long with some sensational beliefs and practices, and sing "ditties" or songs you consider trite or "shallow" on Sunday morning – all without a cynical spirit. You must love people enough to gradually, patiently lift them toward truth, godliness, and excellence! You must be aware of your own weakness and failures.

You've got to associate with the lowly, underprivileged, uneducated, uncouth barbarian without even a twinge of arrogant superiority or self-conscious pride. You'll have to let loose of your pet peeves, your preferences, your tastes, and your securities for the sake of redemption. Some of you will have to take off your suit and tie, while others must be willing to put them on.

Hating your life means developing the mind and heart of a true servant!

I will never forget the time when the Holy Spirit brought into clear focus that I did not possess the heart of a servant.

One afternoon, I walked the short distance to Tim's office with the intent of finding a good book to read. While browsing through his bookshelf, a thin book caught my eye. I picked it up. After leafing through it, I decided to take it home with me. I had barely begun reading Roy Hession's *The Calvary Road* when I sensed a deep unsettling in my spirit. As a matter of fact, I was barely into reading through chapter one, in which the author talks about the necessity of brokenness, that I wanted to slam the book shut and put it away. I was compelled, however, to continue reading. As I read that "yielding to those around us is the true measure of how much we are yielded to God," deep conviction settled down on my heart. I read on: "Every humiliation, everyone who tries and annoys us is God's way of breaking us, so that there is an even deeper channel for the life of Christ to flow in us." I painfully understood that I wasn't broken in my relationship with a certain person. I had allowed differences of opinions and methods to irritate and cause me to chafe in my spirit. I self-righteously believed that I was right and that this person was in error – that if they could somehow get their act together, we could have sweet, unbroken fellowship and a healthy working relationship. **I learned that my inner struggle and lack of peace with God was a result of my own sin.** It was so painful to realize that my own stubborn pride was the real issue and not anything that anyone else had done or could ever do. What relief came when I confessed the condition of my heart and motives to God and asked him to fill me with his love; when I renounced my rights and acknowledged my pride, even confessing this to the other person; when I truly embraced the truth that my lack of peace is never the problem of another, no matter what! At the end of the day, it is my determination to be in control that causes my spirit to be distressed and overwhelmed.

This was a turning point in my life. I have learned that I have to continually lay down my rights. The battle is never completely over. It is a daily choice to love and live in brokenness before God and others.

What will love look like in your life? If you want to have a lasting impact in your place of ministry, whether in your home or on a mission field, you must lay down your rights. You must develop the habit of listening. You will need to cultivate an atmosphere of respect, freedom, and openness. You must be sensitive to cultural traditions. You must equip before establishing expectations or requiring accountability. You must choose your battles wisely. Not every hill is worth dying on. You must work at establishing relationships that are truth based, not just sentimental. These are principles of love. Regarding this last principle, Tim reminds missionaries,

> True love will nurture deep, *Christ-centered* relationships and will avoid building unhealthy dependencies. Love will never

exploit the vulnerable. Love will guard against unhealthy, and even disrespectful, paternalistic relationships – against endearing souls to oneself rather than to Jesus.

People we minister to are often poor, needy, and emotionally broken. It is incumbent on us to be careful about building emotionally dependent relationships. This is a great temptation to Christian workers because these kinds of relationships can feed an emotional need in us. Who doesn't like doting affection? One missionary couple moved to a certain Bible school overseas, and the students *immediately* began referring to them as "Mommy" and "Daddy." I warned this wonderful missionary family that to cultivate or encourage this kind of paternalistic relationship, though tempting, could become a snare. "Mommies and daddies are responsible to care for the needs of their children," I warned. "Are you ready to care for fifty little kids?"

While it is true that Jesus and Paul cultivated deep and affectionate relationships with people to whom and with whom they worked,[1] they always built these relationships on the foundation of obedience to God's Word and the gospel.[2]

Tim and I believe that love is also patient for the true harvest. **Love doesn't press for superficial change**. Love gives time for truth principles to penetrate deep into the heart until they are rooted in culture. Far too many Christian workers spend years, even decades, on superficial transformation (changing outward things) only to realize that when they are no longer able to police people they drift right back to their former practices. Love will do better than this.

We must remember that the Spirit of Jesus is the Spirit of patience. As spouses, parents, and Christian workers, we must cultivate great confidence in the Holy Spirit and the power of the Word of God to bring transformation. Passages like the following must

---

1. 1 Thessalonians 2:6-12 is a great passage to study in this regard.

2. Matthew 12:47-50

continually bring our passions in check: *"And a servant of the Lord must not quarrel but be gentle to all, able to teach, patient, in humility correcting those who are in opposition"* (2 Tim. 2:24-25a).

For every well-planted word there is a season! For every word planted in season there is a fruitful harvest.

Where are you in this matter of love? As you live in community with your family and other believers, what attitudes do differences of opinion and personality stir up in you? In his wonderful book, *The Mind of Christ,* Dennis Kinlaw challenges us with these words:

> A person does not realize this self-centered bent so long as he lives in isolation. One needs to live in community to realize the problems of his own soul. . . . On the foreign mission field, the mission worker's greatest problems are not with the unsaved, but with the other missionaries. That is part of the divine plan. As we serve together in the kingdom, we learn who we are.[1]

As a pastor, pastor's wife, teacher, missionary, or parent, do you find yourself operating from a rigid, heavy-handed, and results-oriented mindset? Do you find it difficult to love those in your life whose actions chafe your spirit like sandpaper? Are you compelled to set about "fixing" what is wrong in the lives of those closest to you and to whom you minister? If this is your mode of operation, especially in the absence divine love, your life and ministry will become nothing more than a burdensome bother. It is true, dear friend, that love "beareth all things, believeth all things, hopeth all things, and endureth all things." And it is only this kind of love that will reap supernatural and enduring results.

---

1. Dennis F. Kinlaw, *The Mind of Christ* (Wilmore: Francis Asbury Press, 1998) 65-6.

CHAPTER EIGHT

Embracing Laughter

A person without a sense of humor is like a wagon without springs. It's jolted by every pebble on the road.
Henry Ward Beecher

Newsflash! Obedience and joy are meant to walk together! *"Serve the Lord with gladness,"* said the Psalmist (Psalm 100:2). Obedience is only half of what God wants. Gladness makes our obedience complete. Delight completes duty.

God must have a marvelous sense of humor because some of the godliest people we know are people whose poverty, burdens, and responsibilities haven't robbed them of their joy or even their sense of humor – people whose joy spills over into laughter because their joy isn't wrapped up in their circumstances or possessions but in their relationship with God.

It's easy for Christian workers to take themselves too seriously. **One of our greatest temptations, in fact, is to develop a "Messiah complex"** – the unhealthy tendency to make ourselves the bearer of every burden, the fix for every problem, the answer to every question, the solution to every dilemma. As Tim and I stepped out in obedience, we found that there were often more people to attend to than time, more burdens than strength, more challenges than wisdom, and more needs than resources. And there was often no shortage of criticism from the very ones whom we were trying to help. Add moving to a cross-cultural environment into the mix, and one could almost forget how to *serve the Lord with gladness.*"

The emotional toll that results from adapting to a new environment – new country, new climate, new culture, new cuisine, new personalities, and a totally new way of doing life – does tend to highlight our solemn side. Navigating survival in a strange new place can sometimes take every bit of intestinal fortitude that we possess, leaving very little room for levity. And, if not careful, we will wake up one morning and realize that we have become stern, humorless, and dour. There have been moments in all our lives when we've become too intense, and our capacity to see the lighter side has been reduced to nothing. Tim and I learned early on in ministry that learning to lighten up and laugh does wonders to strengthen endurance and give joy on the journey.

On that note, I'd like to share a few humorous experiences with you. . .

Living in a strange country was colorful, adventuresome, and brimming with new experiences. I was amazed and sometimes appalled at the ludicrous things that could happen on any given day. One afternoon, I gathered some medical supplies and headed to a nearby village. Tim and one of our ministerial students, Fermin, accompanied me. Tim was the driver, and Fermin agreed to be my interpreter. We traveled down a rutted, dusty road and parked our small van on a ridge, a man-made dike. We walked down a steep, narrow path and through a burned-out corn field to the small cluster of houses beyond. The adults greeted us with a friendly wave and a "Hello, ma'am . . . Hello sir!" while their children peered shyly at us from open doorways. The bravest of the children danced around us on the path as we walked to the center of the village. After spending some time there attending a medical need, we headed back through the corn field towards our vehicle.

Just as we approached the middle of the corn field, Tim suddenly and without warning shoved me in the back and yelled "Run!" In the split second that it took for me to quickly turn my head, I saw out of the corner of my eye a large bull charging right for us! The three of us scattered in all different directions and, for some unknown reason, the bull decided to chase *me*! Terrified, I ran like the wind, my lungs burning and my heart racing! **I dared not stop! The pounding of hooves just behind me prodded me on and on and on.** Just when I thought I was putting some distance between the bull and me, I caught my sandaled foot (hardly the proper running attire) on a leftover corn stalk and went sprawling forward. I knew the bull would be upon me in seconds, so I tried to jump up. Just then, the dreadful beast came to the end of his very long tether! (Even large animals are usually staked in the Philippines.) I glanced behind me and saw him, just a few feet away, pawing the ground and snorting angrily! As I stood up shakily and brushed myself off, I looked back to see if any of the villagers had watched the drama. To my profound embarrassment, some were lined up in front of their houses and had caught the whole event. They laughed and waved wildly! I swallowed my humiliation and managed a shaky arm motion in their direction. I walked to where Tim and Fermin stood catching their breath. They were both relieved and tried to express genuine concern for me, but they didn't do well at concealing their amusement! Tim had to nearly carry me to the car. My knees were so weak that I could barely walk. I laid awake that night unable to sleep. Each time I closed my eyes, I saw the bull and relived in vivid detail the terrifying rendition of my personal "run of the bulls."

A few days later I returned to the village, secretly hoping that they had forgotten the whole scene. They hadn't! They looked at me with broad grins, and one of them said, "Ma'am, you run very fast!" I suddenly saw the humor in what they must have witnessed. This strange white woman running like mad with her long multicolored skirt flapping in the breeze. I began laughing out loud, and they were quick to join me. These villagers were probably amazed not only that this Americano actually came back, but that I was able to laugh at myself. In the end, the whole event may have even helped to open the door a little bit more in that spiritually dark place. *She's human after all! And she can laugh about it!*

After moving to the Philippines, **I learned very quickly that there was someone in our family who possessed an even greater aversion to "creeping things" (like rodents) than I.** Tim, my strong and *brave* husband, could barely bring himself to face down these little critters. This was both funny and surprising to me. We had been married for more than twelve years, and I had never known about his creepy-crawly phobia. Tim could be fearless when it came to traveling, eating strange and exotic foods, and sleeping in unconventional places; but the critters could turn him into a . . . well . . . *different* person!

For example, one night a *harmless* little lizard found a cozy place to sleep in our bed. We were unaware of it until it ran up Tim's leg. Pure pandemonium broke out. It was very funny!

Another time, we took a birthday trip with then thirteen-year-old Valerie. We packed up our van and, leaving our boys with the Blacks, headed for Baguio city, a tourist city about two hours north and about five thousand feet up the mountains.

We had only made it about a mile down the road when a very fat rat fell from under the dash directly onto Tim's right leg. Even through his jeans, he felt its little claws digging into skin as it struggled for something to hold on to! Suddenly, the car careened off the road; Tim's legs came off the pedals; and he screamed . . . like a *woman*! We all exited the car with breakneck speed. Tim looked under the car and under the dash trying to find this unwelcome passenger (who had evidently crawled back to his hiding place in the dash), but we couldn't find him. We finally agreed that in all the confusion the rat must have jumped out of the van and run into the adjacent field. We just hadn't seen him go. So, we climbed rather reluctantly back into the vehicle (I chose to sit in the back with Valerie this time) and started out again. It wasn't five minutes later that the little gray monster poked his fat head out of a hole in the dash, and his nose touched Tim's knee. His knees came up and, once again, I heard this unnatural, womanish yell! He jerked the car unceremoniously off the road for the second time. As we piled out of the van, Tim announced that we'd be staying by the road until *he* witnessed the exiting of the stowaway! We opened all four doors; and after several minutes, we saw the rat jump down and waddle off into the weeds, oblivious I'm sure to the extreme duress he had caused these skittish Americans. After we stopped shaking, Tim and I laughed for days! And with each retelling of this little drama, we relive the humor of those moments.

When faced with something that to us seemed incompatible with reality – you know, those "Dorothy, you're not in Kansas anymore" moments, laughter was our shock absorber. On some levels it was refreshing to view life outside of our own small, narrow comfort zone. It certainly kept things interesting.

We attended many weddings during our years in the Philippines. These were fun and culturally colorful events. We always enjoyed participating in the celebrations.

On one occasion, we traveled about seven hours up into the mountains to attend the wedding of two of our Bible college students. We arrived the evening before and joined in for the food and festivities. After dinner, we all sat around in a small clearing near the bride's house and watched as friends and family members sang, gave speeches, and celebrated the impending marriage of this couple. At one point in the evening, it was announced that they would now be performing the Ifugao native dance. Soon, young and old alike began forming a circle around the roaring bonfire located in the middle of the clearing. I was amused and delighted to see one of the men grab my husband by the hand and pull him into the group of native dancers. Tim was a great sport; but knowing him as I do, it was great fun to witness his embarrassment as he reluctantly joined the group. **I laughed and laughed as I watched him hop around the fire on one foot, slightly bent forward, arms outstretched, trying his best to emulate what the others were doing**. My only regret was that I did not capture this moment on camera. I'm quite sure they didn't train him for this in Bible college! I was not so amused, however, when a moment later, they came looking for me. I declined politely, using my advanced state of pregnancy as an excuse!

Later on that evening, as we sat talking, someone mentioned to me that there was a family member of the bride who was mentally ill. They said that he was tied to a tree behind the house. This was shocking to me, and even more so when they went on to say that the family had him restrained because he refused to keep his clothes on. It also saddened me to know that this was the only way the family could deal with him. I must admit, however, that my mind conjured up a mental picture of the scene should the poor man somehow get loose and show up at the wedding.

After a lovely ceremony the following morning, we made our way to the bride's home for the wedding feast. We sat in the heat, under a large tent and enjoyed various dishes made with pork, vegetables, rice, and fresh fruit. We washed it all down with warm bottles of sweet Pop Cola. Suddenly, fifteen-year-olds Valerie and Roanna came running to me with panicked expressions. Roanna was the first to find her voice. "Aunt Becky!" she hissed, "there's a naked man walking around!" They were absolutely dumbfounded and a bit traumatized, to put it mildly. I realized that the family member of the bride had, indeed, managed to extricate himself from his bonds. The most amazing thing about this was that we, the Americanos, were the only ones staring at him. The others politely pretended that it was perfectly normal for a thirty-year-old man to be walking around in the nude.

I've always been told that there is a lesson to be learned in every situation. Perhaps the truth gleaned from this bizarre event was that when the unthinkable happens and it can't be helped, then spare those involved embarrassment and look away. As for our two teenage girls, they are both healthy, well-adjusted adult women today and are no worse for the experience. I'm sure, however, that they've never forgotten it!

Tim and I had heard through the grapevine that the Shepherd's College boys would often have late night "barbeques." We knew that these nocturnal feasts consisted of sundry stray animals that they could find – birds, snakes, rats, and the occasional stray cat. One evening Tim walked outside and found our golden retriever, Buddy, tossing a round object into the air with his mouth and then rolling on it. It looked like a small black ball, but he hadn't remembered the children having one. Curious, he walked closer and realized to his astonishment that it was a blackened, charcoaled cats head! It didn't take him long to figure out where it had come from, so he decided to have a little fun. He walked over to the college cafeteria where the students were finishing up their meal. The remains of a cooking fire smoldered nearby. Tim greeted them and nonchalantly asked, "Hey guys, have you seen a small cat...?" While they stared with wide, questioning eyes, he went on, "Yeah, I bought my kids a little cat to play with, and we can't find it anywhere. Have you all seen it?" The students stopped eating and looked back at Tim with stricken faces. Finally, one of them found his voice. "Uh ... what color was it, sir?" he asked weakly. "Well, right now it's black, and my dog is playing with its head," Tim answered playfully. And then he simply couldn't restrain his laughter any longer! He told the young men he knew what they'd been up to, and as he laughed a look of relief washed over the students' faces. They all began to laugh, greatly relieved that they hadn't eaten the missionary's pet.

Laughter that bursts forth from a cheerful heart *really* is good medicine. It's medicine for our souls. It's medicine for our relationships. Cheerfulness is maintained through humility – a commitment to vulnerability. **Cheerfulness has power to heal relationships and remove cultural, economic, and social barriers.** Storytelling helps us know one another. Vulnerability breaks down walls! Tim and I think that taking the time to share life's ironic, awkward, humorous, and, yes, even painful moments has an amazing way of binding hearts together, of leveling the playing field and making us one.

We found that Filipinos love to laugh . . . often during the most tragic moments. Perhaps it's their way of coping and healing. As our family traveled life's road of obedience together with them, there were many awkward moments dissolved when we each relaxed and laughed at each other's feeble attempts to bridge the gaps between our worlds. We found acceptance when we learned to throw off expectations and enjoy our common humanity so creatively woven like a brilliant thread through our diverse cultures. Victor Borge was on to something when he said, ***"Laughter is the shortest distance between two people."***

I smile even now when I think of the many laughs we must have supplied to our patient and fun-loving Filipino friends and coworkers. Watching our uproariously funny language blunders (these can't be put into print) or standing anxiously by and seeing our faces as we tried new and never-before-eaten foods surely must have them still talking . . . and laughing. In our years of working with them, we learned that dedication to Christ isn't sanctimonious, that sacrifice isn't incompatible with joy, and that devotion isn't dull and dour. We learned that cheerfulness and laughter are surely the marks of sincere, trusting discipleship.

A merry heart does good, like medicine, but a broken spirit dries the bones (Proverbs 17:22).

Our first Sunday in the Philippines, October 1996

Valerie and Timothy posing in front of our Charlie Brown tree on our first Christmas in the Philippines

First washing machine!

John Parker teaching Timothy to play the guitar

John Parker and Tim, hiking to a new church plant

Becky and Timothy after Bible study in Casareno

Tim and David Yuccadi (right) in 2002, with Bro. Andres

Keep family with kids' furry friends, 2002

Left: Becky and baby Mark

Above: Jasmine and Mark

Becky and Christina (Black) with helpers, Rowena (left) and Virgie (center)

Timothy riding the tractor!

Valerie with a village girl

Above: Deron Fourman (back), Tim, Timothy, and David Black (front)

Left: Sam and Carrie with campus friends

Right: Valerie and campus friends

Valerie and Timothy with friends

Medical mission in the remote village of Caritas

Hiking to a medical mission

This is how Jesse was able to hike the terraces safely!

Taking a break on the trail

Carrie and Sam conducting their own medical mission!

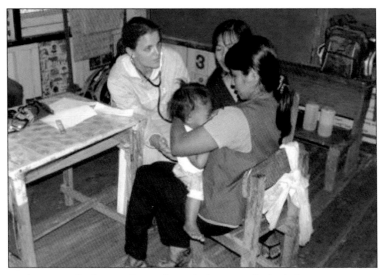

Becky, treating patients during a medical mission

Becky teaching Basic Health and Hygiene

This eighty-year-old woman passed us on the trail

The Keep kids during vacation in Puerto Galera

Our new home in the Philippines after the first one was finally torn down

Keep kids and friends riding atop the jeepney

Jesse and campus kids having fun

The Old Woman

The little girls learning to squat like their friends

Tim preaching with Alice Dolteo interpreting

Tim, Deron Fourman, Timothy, John Parker and Pastor Oncie Undo hiking to a Bible conference

Valerie and Jesse with Filipino friends

Valerie with great MK friend, Roanna Black

Tim and Becky helping in the Filipino wedding of Rojelio and Rowena

Our farewell service, April 2009

The Keep family today

CHAPTER NINE

The Poor Made Rich through the Gospel

*Listen, my beloved brethren: has God not chosen the poor of
this world to be rich in faith and heirs of the kingdom
which he promised to those who love him?*
James 2:5

Obedience to God in spite of temporal hardships points to the power of the gospel and to Christ's surpassing, eternal worth. Like many young missionaries, Tim and I went to the Philippines fully expecting to jump in and *serve* wherever we could. We were zealous to begin the work God had called us to. We were ready to *do* ... to *give* ... to *teach* these needy people. As we began building relationships, the "*Filipinos*" soon became *individuals* – unique individuals with names, faces, families, gifts, emotions, and ... hurts! As our family worshiped, worked, and played side by side with them, the Lord began to enlarge our hearts with love. As Tim and I began *listening more* and *talking less,* we began to discover rich qualities of faith lying beneath the surface of their often simple, unassuming personalities. Soon, *we* became the students and *they* the teachers. *We* were the ones being served. *We* were the ones being instructed!

As we observed their quiet faith and living hope through some of the most difficult circumstances imaginable, we realized that we had much to learn about following Jesus. We learned that the gospel is truly the power of God unto salvation, and that it alone can meet mankind's *deepest* needs.

I met Rufina only days after our arrival in the Philippines. I was wandering around the mission house in a daze, trying to acclimate myself to the heat and to push past the exhaustion I felt from having traveled halfway around the world with two small children.

I heard a light knock on the screen door and looked up to see a tiny Filipino girl with lovely long, black, silky hair that hung below her waist. She smiled shyly and said simply, "I will be the one to help you ma'am." Though a bit taken back, I opened the door and beckoned for her to come inside. In a matter of moments, Rufina was moving quickly and efficiently – sweeping floors, cleaning out cupboards, and washing dishes. In no time at all, she had helped me to get things in order.

Rufina's English was quite good, and I learned that she was a Shepherd's College student. She was married to Rogelio, who had already finished his studies and was currently working as the campus maintenance man. They lived together in a small house just next to ours; and though they had no children of their own, they cared for Rogelio's niece whose mother was working overseas. This young three-year-old became an instant playmate to our children.

Each Saturday morning, I would watch as Rogelio and Rufina left the campus on an old motorcycle. Rogelio would drive, and Rufina would sit delicately perched sidesaddle on the back with one hand resting comfortably on Rogelio's shoulder. I wondered how in the world she managed to stay put in that position! Late Sunday afternoon, the two would return. I learned that Rogelio and Rufina were pioneering a little church plant in Maburac, a village about ten kilometers away. The Lord was blessing their ministry, and they already had a thriving group of believers. Their practice was to spend Saturday afternoons visiting the villagers of Maburac, praying in their homes, conducting Bible studies, and fellowshipping. Both Rogelio and Rufina took the shepherding of their little flock very seriously.

This couple remained faithful, and we watched as the congregation grew and eventually a church building and parsonage were built. After Rufina's graduation from the Shepherd's College, she and Rogelio packed up their few belongings and moved into the tiny parsonage. The church and village of Maburac now became their full time passion.

God blessed Rogelio and Rufina greatly in their ministry, but they had one desire that eluded them: they longed for a child. After many years of marriage, it became apparent that apart from a miracle this longing would never be fulfilled. Rufina suffered some health issues and had even undergone a major surgery to remove a goiter. Although she had recovered, she was never quite as strong. Soon after the surgery, it was discovered that her heart was severely damaged. We took her to Manila to be examined by a reputable heart surgeon; he was shocked at her condition, making it clear that her only hope for survival was to have a mitral valve replacement.

Rufina weakened daily. Each time I visited her, her breathing was more rapid and labored. She grew painfully thin, and the rich brown tone of her skin paled. She continued faithfully working in the church alongside her husband, and God continued to bring a rich harvest of souls.

Finally, we were able to get a surgery date for Rufina. It was an early morning in late July that we loaded up our van with Rufina, Rogelio, and several family members to make the trip to Manila. Rufina was nervous but very optimistic. She was excited at this chance to live. I will never forget accompanying her to her hospital room. The nurse just outside the door motioned for her to step up onto a scale. As she did so, I peered over her shoulder, curious to see how much she weighed. Rufina laughed when she saw that she tipped the scales at a mere 78 lbs. I laughed with her but was sobered by how great a toll this illness had already taken on her body.

I sat with her in her room for a while. She was scheduled for early the next morning. We chatted about many things, including her longing to have a baby. She was hopeful because the doctor had told her that she could very possibly conceive after her body had recovered from this surgery. If it had been possible, I would have hidden my own swollen belly. I was four weeks away from giving birth to my fifth child. It didn't seem fair.

As Tim and I prepared to leave so that Rufina could rest and also spend some time alone with her mother and husband, we bowed our heads to pray. Before we began, however, Rufina spoke up. She spoke of her gratitude for those who had provided her this opportunity. She talked of her hope that this surgery would be successful and bring healing to her body. But her final words to us were unforgettable: **"But, no matter what happens tomorrow,"** she said, **"my testimony is Philippians 1:21: 'For me to live is Christ, and to die is gain.' I am resigned to the will of God for my life."**

When I saw her the morning after her surgery, she whispered to me to please extend her thanks to her brothers and sisters in America who had given sacrificially so that she could undergo her operation. I assured her that I would.

On the second morning after Rufina's surgery, I received a call from the surgeon. He told me regretfully that Rufina had just slipped from this world and into the next. Her body was just too fragile to make the recovery.

I wept. I was overwhelmed with sadness that this story did not end differently. I wondered why God had allowed such a faithful servant to leave this world at the age of thirty-three. My heart ached for her husband and stepdaughter who would have to continue life without her. I learned that there are some things in life that we will never be able to "qualify" with our finite rationale.

As we celebrated her life and mourned her death, God was glorified over and over through the testimonies of those whose lives she had impacted for eternity. As I listened, I realized that while Rufina had never known the joy of birthing her own child, she had been the spiritual mother of many. I realized that though poor in this world, Rufina was extravagantly rich in faith, and that her life and testimony would live on through the eternal investments she had carefully made during her few years on this earth.

Rufina's eternal perspective had caused her to treasure eternal things, and her obedience to God's will led to the salvation of many. The rewards of obedience are eternal!

Rufina, as well as many of our national coworkers, pointed our family to the power of the gospel: not only to save from the deepest sins, but to also produce songs in the darkest nights; to produce spiritual abundance – humble acceptance, serenity, contentment – in life's most trying moments. We've been enriched beyond measure by their unwavering obedience in the midst of trial.

I challenge you to open your eyes to the power of the gospel at work in the lives of "ordinary" believers around you. **The greatest blessings you will ever receive will flow from unlikely people, in the most unlikely places, whose stories of grace will spill over into your own life, adding immeasurable hope and courage**.

———————————

About two weeks after returning to the Philippines in 2002, our local pastor's wife, Sis. Alona, came to me with a request. There was a young teenage boy of our campus congregation named Emil who had become very sick. Sis. Alona asked if I would agree to visit him at his home. The next day found me walking across the street and down a dirt path which led to the back door of their simple concrete block house. I paused for a moment and then knocked somewhat timidly, calling out softly, "Apo," as I did so.

Emil's mother, Aida, answered the door and with a worried but grateful expression on her face motioned for me to come inside. I followed her into the "sala" (living room). It was small with a bare, smooth cement floor and low ceilings. An opening in one wall served as a window. There was no glass, and the mint green curtains blew gently as the hot, late afternoon breeze swept into the room.

My eyes were drawn to the narrow bamboo bed positioned under the window and to the young boy lying there. My heart skipped a beat as I grappled with the instant realization that *this boy isn't sick, this boy is dying*! I tried to keep the alarm from showing on my face as I walked closer and took in his emaciated form – long, thin arms and skeletal legs showing beneath a thin blanket. Most shocking, perhaps, was that his head and face were disproportionally large in comparison to the rest of his body. His neck was enormous and bulging with lumpy masses. He was quiet, and his large brown eyes followed me as I stepped closer and managed to smile and introduce myself. He smiled weakly but did not speak.

As I talked to Emil's mother, I was distressed that she had no idea what was wrong with her son. I learned that he had become ill five months earlier. Aida and her husband, Lando, had taken Emil to a doctor who had told them to take him home and care for him. I asked her if the doctor had given them any papers when they left the hospital. She scurried away and ten minutes later came back with some crumpled hospital discharge papers. I read them and discovered that Emil was fourteen years of age and that he had been diagnosed with nasopharyngeal carcinoma (a malignant cancer of the throat) stage IV. This diagnosis was months old, and he had not received even the first treatment. I gathered from talking to Emil's mother that she believed he would recover. This is what she had understood from the doctor. I was stunned!

I left their home with a sick feeling in my stomach. This child was not going to survive – of this I was sure. It seemed so unfair! I wondered, *did the doctor who diagnosed Emil purposely shield his parents from the truth? And if so, did he do so because he knew that they had no money for treatment? Did he do this out of compassion, thinking that if they didn't know then perhaps it would be easier for them to accept his death?*

My mind raced back to the very recent past and our own experience with childhood cancer. I winced as I thought of the fact that in America a child in Emil's economic position would most certainly be granted a chance at life. The inequality of this whole situation pressed down upon me, leaving me depressed and anxious. Later that evening, as I tucked my now healthy and energetic four-year-old Jesse into bed, I was overcome with both gratitude and guilt for our good fortune. I remembered too well the years of expert care he had been given, without which he would never have survived his own fight with cancer. As I kissed him and held him just a bit tighter, I thought of Emil's mom and how the love she and I both had for our boys was a bond we shared that no cultural divide could sever.

For several months, I visited daily and offered whatever help I could. Emil endured unspeakable suffering; and I witnessed his parents' tears as they looked on sadly, helpless to relieve him. I was able to obtain a prescription for strong pain medication. This helped some, but it felt miniscule in comparison to what he really needed.

I spent a great deal of time with Aida and Lando and learned about Emil through them. He loved Jesus and had dreamed of attending our Shepherd's College and becoming a pastor. He loved basketball and music. There were many days when the young people – ours, the children of our coworkers, and our church youth group – would visit Emil. They would sing; and while we worshiped, silent tears would often slide down Emil's pale cheeks as the Holy Spirit filled that little room with his presence.

Emil's condition worsened. Late one evening in early May, my phone rang. I answered and recognized Aida's voice on the line. She was crying. "Emil can't breathe!" she repeated over and over. Tim and I quickly dressed and hurried over. It appeared that Emil was dying. His eyes were open wide, and he was gasping for every breath. It was a dreadful scene. The room was stifling hot, his mother was crying, and his father stood beside his son's bed wearing a look of helpless terror. Tim and I quickly decided to transport Emil to the local clinic. I felt that we could at least get some oxygen for him, which would make his final moments a bit easier.

Tim backed our mission jeep up to the house; and Emil was gently carried by his dad, Tim, and brothers to the back, where they laid him on a foam mattress. I joined his mother and dad in the back for the short ride to the clinic. It was silent except for Emil's pitiful gasping, until I heard something else. I thought he was trying to speak. I leaned over in the darkness in an attempt to hear and realized with disbelief that he was singing. I could scarcely believe my ears! This boy, who moments before was gasping for every breath, was now singing! The words were soft but clear: "*My heart's desire is to bless your holy name, my heart's desire is to lift you up today, even in the time of trial, even in the time of trouble my heart's desire is to bless your holy name.*"[1]

As we all listened in awe, Emil continued to sing: "*Jesus, name above all names, beautiful Savior, glorious Lord, Emmanuel, God is with us, blessed Redeemer, living Word.*"[2] Tears flooded our eyes as we listened and as God's presence filled that jeep. I felt that I had entered a sacred place and was privileged beyond measure to witness the immensity of God's powerful grace being poured out to this precious boy in direct proportion to his suffering.

---

1. Author not found.

2. Hearn, Naida. "Jesus, name above all names." Lyrics. Scripture in Song (admin. by Maranatha Music), 1978.

It was only a few days later that we stood singing as Emil breathed his last and was released from his diseased and pain-riddled body straight into the presence of God.

I have pondered those last four months of Emil's life many times and have experienced a myriad of emotions. I have been pierced by guilt that my son survived cancer and Emil did not. I have felt the pang of regret that I was unable to do more. I have wrestled with anger toward a government system which denies a chance at life simply because of poverty. I have felt profound sadness for parents whose teenage son was snatched away in his youth. I have felt admiration for them for so lovingly caring for him right up to the end.

But Emil also helped us understand what it really means to be "rich." **While he had nothing in this world, while he wasted away physically, he flourished and thrived in God.** This was Emil's true wealth – wealth that nothing nor anyone could take from him. I understood powerfully that the money, time, and prayer expended by so many to train the pastors and Christian workers in our local church was an investment whose returns were infinite. I remembered that it was through these faithful workers that Emil heard the gospel and received eternal life. I witnessed that in the absence of physical succor, the God of all comfort was giving himself to his own with reckless abandon. God held nothing back, and what he gave was immeasurably more than anything money could have bought for this dying boy.

As missionaries, ministers, Christian workers, and even Christian neighbors, we must never forget the absolute power of the gospel. And we must never neglect this irreplaceable treasure. While we *must* relieve suffering where we can – feeding the hungry, clothing the naked, caring for orphans and widows – we must never forget that these humanitarian endeavors without the gospel will only have a *temporal* impact. Humanitarian relief is never an end. Our deepest needs and the deepest needs of the poor and suffering around the world can only be satisfied in the gospel!

Apart from the eternal hope of the gospel, the immensity of the needs all around us will overwhelm us, and our feeble attempts to relieve temporal suffering will always fall short. Unless we are sharing the gospel, too, we are only treating symptoms while leaving the disease untouched. Where Jesus is received he becomes the forgiver of sin, a Father to the fatherless, a Husband to lonely widows, Living Water for thirsty souls, Bread of Life for the hungry, and The Great Physician for the suffering. Where the gospel is preached to the poor, sin's captives are set free, the suffering rejoice in their temporary afflictions, the weak are endued with strength, and the hopeless are filled with assurance and eternal consolation. We must never water down the gospel or replace it with social action, for *"it is the power of God unto salvation to everyone who believes"* (Romans 1:16).

May I ask you, my friend, what difference is the gospel of Jesus Christ making in your own life?

CHAPTER TEN

Obedience Is a Family Affair

*And if it seems evil to you to serve the LORD, choose for yourselves this day whom you will serve, whether the gods which your fathers served that were on the other side of the River, or the gods of the Amorites, in whose land you dwell. **But as for me and my house, we will serve the LORD.***
Joshua 24:15 *(Emphasis added)*

There is no better training for children than to be included in their parent's obedience.

When Tim and I uprooted our little family from our American life, we had no idea what our new reality would look like. In those early days, I could never have imagined that I would give birth to three children in that faraway place. I never dreamed that because of power outages, hot afternoons would find me bathing my kids at an outdoor pump well. Nor had I envisioned taking our five children, one blind and two under the age of five, on jolting jeepney rides (the luxury of car seats and seatbelts long forgotten) through the mountains or hiking for hours through a rain forest to conduct medical missions in remote villages. After all, I was an American mom. There was a very real part of me that desired for my kids all the "familiar" activities which accompany growing up in the USA. It was not without some trepidation that I surrendered to the fact that my children would experience a "different" reality than their cousins and friends back home. I sometimes grieved just a bit over what I perceived they were missing out on.

Obedience will always cost those closest to us. Oswald Chambers said: "If we obey God, it is going to cost other people more than it costs us, and that is where the pain begins" (*My Utmost for His Highest,* Jan 11th). Perhaps this is the greatest test of our surrender. Chambers then goes on to say: "If we obey God, he will care for those who have suffered the consequences of our obedience." I must admit I was afraid at times that my obedience would cost my kids too much and affect them negatively in some way – that they might become bitter and resentful of their perceived, and sometimes real, losses brought about by our obedience.

I feel certain that our obedience to God, though not without a price, will always (although perhaps not immediately) benefit our children. *Satan's* greatest fear may be that our children will witness through our obedience just how true, faithful, and trustworthy God really is; so he preys upon *our* parental fears. What better way to cement eternal truth into the lives of our kids than to allow them to see firsthand the power of God at work in and through the obedience of their parents. So, it should come as no surprise that Satan often overwhelms those who embrace ministry with fear or pity for their children – to believe that the lives of their kids will be sabotaged by their faithfulness to God.

Honestly, there were times when Tim and I were tempted by these thoughts. Our kids' lives were not without struggle. They did suffer some deprivations they would not have experienced had we chosen not to live in the third world. But as we lived, loved, worked, prayed, and ministered together as a family unit, we were often surprised and delighted at all the interesting adventures missionary life offered.

Our kids were not miniature super-saints, nor did we expect them to be perfect little MKs. Trust me, they never were! We were amazed, however, to witness their readiness to jump in and help with different ministries we were involved in. Tim and I loved our work, and it was so much fun to be able to include our kids in what we were doing.

We conducted at least fifteen medical missions during our stay in the Philippines. The kids absolutely loved this! I gave Tim Jr. a lesson on how to give injections, and he gave hundreds of life-saving immunizations to children and adults throughout remote villages. Jesse handed out candy after the deed was done to soothe the tears that followed. Valerie especially loved working with our volunteer dentist from Manila. She assisted Dr. Wawi, who pulled hundreds of infected teeth, easing the suffering of many. When the little girls, Carrie and Sammi, were along, they weren't much help but did provide lots of entertainment. Tim and I didn't want our children to be shielded from the devastating poverty and injustice which exists in much of the world. **Our constant prayer has been that through their exposure to the raw suffering of so many, a seed of compassion for a lost and hurting world would be lodged deep in their hearts**. Our greatest desire is that this seed will blossom into a life of ministry and that wherever God places them, they will always notice – really notice – the sorely wounded around them and be ready and willing to make a difference.

Tim would often take the boys with him as he traveled to our churches deep into the mountains. Jesse had picked up playing the king flute (a native Filipino instrument), and Timothy was always ready with his guitar. They'd play for congregations small and large scattered throughout those villages. They bathed in the river with Dad, played with the village children, sampled all sorts of exotic foods – not the least being snake, dog, and goat intestines. They drank coconut milk straight from the coconut and often sat under mango trees eating green mango dipped in salt and vinegar.

Timothy enjoys the memory of a piggy back ride from one of our pastors as they crossed a river that would have been just a bit deep for him to manage on his own.

We were gently admonished by older and wiser missionaries to avoid neglecting the needs of our family. We are so grateful for this wisdom. We did find that if we weren't intentionally attentive, we'd find ourselves giving precedence to others at the expense of our own family, especially when their needs seemed to be so much more pressing than ours.

We purposely took special time away to rest and focus on each other and our kids. Honestly, it wasn't without some guilt in the beginning. I mean, we were here to sacrifice and serve. How could we possibly spend money and time on a vacation? We are convinced, however, that those getaways were ordered of the Lord and vital to the health and well-being of our family.

The road of obedience for us was much more than struggle and sacrifice. We discovered beautiful vacation spots in the tropical islands that were incredibly affordable. We enjoyed the beauty of the country where God had called us to serve.

One of our greatest memories as a family is traveling to the southern island of Mindoro for a week of sun and sand. It was an unforgettable adventure after a long and particularly busy season of ministry! We traveled by bus for five hours to the southern part of Manila. We then bought tickets for the two hour "ferry" boat ride to the island. We walked a narrow plank to board this small dilapidated homemade boat. I was amused at what a novelty our fair-skinned kids were as we traveled. The little girls, then two and four, soon grew weary of their cheeks being pinched and their hair tousled by friendly, curious Filipinos.

After crossing the Philippine Sea, our boat ride carried us along an amazing channel flanked by thousands of coconut palms. We were deposited onto a beautiful tropical beach in the village of Puerto Galera where a mob of tricycle drivers clamored for the chance to take us to our seaside resort. We were pleasantly surprised with the accommodations we had booked sight unseen and spent seven delightful days building sand castles, playing volleyball, and snorkeling in the Philippine Sea. We enjoyed a picnic each day in our own private Nipa hut. Tim and I spent lazy afternoons resting under the shade of a coconut palm, devouring thick novels while the kids played nearby. Each evening, we dined in a small café situated on the beach with brilliant sunsets as our backdrop. Later, as the sun sank lower into the horizon, our little girls chased small spidery crabs that skittered across the sand while Tim and I challenged the older children in games of ping pong. After long, full, but relaxing days, we all slept soundly. This was a great place to reconnect with each other away from the demands of ministry.

At week's end, we headed for home. We were tired, sunburned, and carrying suitcases laden with salty, sandy laundry; but we also carried with us happy hearts and rested spirits. These days, and others like them throughout our years in the Philippines, did wonders to fortify us mentally, physically, relationally, and even spiritually. God is truly the giver of so much good to those who follow him.

I don't want to leave the impression, however, that life was divided equally between intense ministry and play. Perhaps life is more appealing for many of us when we're in the middle of some large and important project or an exciting adventure. **Most of missionary life was for me, as a wife and mother, simply lived in the realm of the mundane. Sometimes it was even downright dull!** I found that being consistent and faithful – with a good attitude – in the gritty minutiae of life was often my greatest challenge. It is still my greatest challenge!

When we moved to the Philippines in 1996, we had two children, ages five and two. Over the course of the next nine years, God blessed us with another son and two little girls. Like mothers all over the world, my days were a dizzying cycle of laundry, "marketing," cooking, and overseeing the education of the children. These are daunting tasks, even in one's comfort zone where everything is familiar and convenient. I was often overwhelmed just trying to keep up while having to adjust my methods and make things work in this sometimes strange (to me) and new environment.

After our first year, things became a bit easier as the old mission house (which was falling down around us) was replaced with a new and much more efficient one. This house was built while we were home for Jesse's cancer treatments. It was large with five bedrooms (two of them guest rooms) and three baths, and I was so grateful for the ceramic tiled floors throughout. They were cleanable, and I felt comfortable about my babies crawling around on them. The living/kitchen area was a spacious open floor plan, a great place to entertain. The house sported a large front porch which was covered and tiled. This was a perfect place for the kids to play on rainy days. There was a side porch, also covered, which provided shelter for our vehicle. It was also an ideal shady spot for the small swimming pool I found in the market. Our two youngest and many of their friends spent long sweltering afternoons splashing around in it in an effort to stay cool. From the kitchen door, we walked into an enclosed back porch. This served as our laundry room. There was ample space to hang clothes and also a door leading to a small outside porch and a clothesline.

Although the house was cement, it was still blistering hot inside. In the beginning, we purchased a small air conditioner for our bedroom. This became the family "hangout" of sorts. We called it "The Cave"! Eventually, we were able to purchase a larger unit to place in the main living area. It was enough to cut the humidity in the house and bring the temperature down to a bearable one. I think our thermostat usually read around 85 degrees on most days. The cost of electricity was so astronomical, however, that after a few months, my husband informed me that I had to choose between using my clothes dryer or my air conditioner. It may have been a difficult decision for me had I not been very pregnant with my fourth child. I simply could not manage without the air conditioning.

I had never had to hang laundry outside before in my life, but I discovered something calming and relaxing about this mundane chore. I'd get up early and start the laundry each day at 6:00 a.m. My goal was to have it all on the line by 10:00 a.m. It dried quickly in the scorching tropical heat, and I'd fluff it only for a few minutes in the dryer to remove a little of the stiffness.

Hanging laundry reminded me of my grandmother. I'd seen her do this so many times, and I always loved the smell of her bed sheets. She had wanted so badly to be a missionary but had been married and widowed while very young. She raised five children, and missionary life was impossible for her. I remembered her excitement when she learned that Tim and I were going to be missionaries. It occurred to me that her dream of being a missionary was being lived out through me. As I stood feeling the sun burning my face and arms, I felt connected to her through this menial familiar task that she and I shared. Although decades later and ten thousand miles away, I was doing the same thing that she had done, although her life had been vastly different than my own.

One of the great blessings of daily life in the Philippines was having someone to help me with housework. There was so much dust and dirt filtering through our steel-framed windows that our house needed a good daily cleaning. The tile in the house, although lovely, was white, shiny, and very high maintenance – doubly so as we had so many children traipsing in and out all day long. The floor had to be mopped daily. Valerie was an amazing help with this but earned the name "Cinderella" because it seemed that all she did was help with cleaning the house!

In the beginning, the Bible college students would help me during their work hour in the afternoon. By the time I was expecting our fourth child, however, it became evident that we needed more full-time help. The Lord sent that help in the person of Rowena. She was a quiet but sweet and extremely efficient girl who became like part of our family. She worked for twenty hours each week and was such a blessing to all of us. I also found that she was an amazing cook, and she would cook for me on occasion. I cared for the kids, did the laundry and most of the cooking. Rowena kept the house clean and sanitary. We were a great team.

Each week, it was also my job to do the marketing for the family. This was no small undertaking, but it was also a day that I looked forward to. It was my "mom's day out."

We were blessed to have wonderful coworkers, David and Christina Black, and their children, Robert and Roanna. Christina and I would go together each week, armed with our shopping lists and menus. This was usually about a six-hour ordeal. We laughingly dubbed it our "foraging for food" outing. We'd go from store to store, sometimes driving over an hour to find the needed items. We made the most of the day. We shared about our lives, needs, and frustrations; and we laughed a lot! We'd usually enjoy lunch at McDonalds or even KFC, and often we'd top the day off with a delicious Filipino dessert called "Halo Halo." This consisted of a large glass of shaved ice which was filled with different fruits and even sweet beans. They'd pour in some evaporated milk, leche flan, a slab of purple ube plant (similar to sweet potato), and top it off with ice cream and granola. This cold, sweet, calorie-laden treat was refreshing and fortifying for two missionary ladies who had endured a long day of shopping in the extreme heat.

I slowly learned that the key to embracing a new life, a new normal, and new set of circumstances was to do just that – embrace it! Our normal reaction to change is usually to chafe against it – to resist it, to pine for how things used to be, to wish the familiar back. It is so easy to jump into new situations and immediately go about "fixing" them to meet our expectations. I found this exhausting. Little by little, the Lord taught me to bend my expectations, to lean into our new culture, and to even learn to savor its unique "flavors"! This was part of my lesson in obedience.

Upon returning to the Philippines in February of 2002, we were delighted not only with the new mission house, but with a new and nearly-completed college administration building. This building was located right beside our home and had replaced a tired and dilapidated boy's dorm. It was a lovely two-story building which housed both missionary and college offices and several classrooms. Along the front of the building was a full-length porch.

Within a day of arriving on campus, I noticed an old woman who appeared to be "camping out" on that porch. She had an old rice sack bulging with her belongings and another rice sack or two which she draped from the railing to serve as a shelter of sorts. After asking around, Tim and I learned that she had been there for quite some time. We learned that her family resided across the street and that she suffered dementia. The story was that she had a son who had left years earlier to work in Spain. He promised his mother that he would come home and build a house for her. When she noticed the big beautiful building going up on our campus, she believed it to be the home that her son had promised. She brought her things and moved in. Although they tried, her family could not persuade her to come home. Once a day she would walk across the street to her family to get food, but she spent nearly all her days and nights sitting there on her rice sacks on the porch of our administration building.

I was horrified by this at first. It was so strange and seemed so wrong. Tim approached one of our senior college administrators and asked what could be done for this woman. He replied, "She is old, so we will just let her stay if she likes. It's no problem." Everything in me wanted to rectify this situation. Occasionally, I would see her bathing at night. She would do this using the pump well located in the middle of our campus. She would sometimes sit on the swings and sing loudly for long periods of time. I wanted to bring her inside, give her a hot shower, feed her something, and secure a permanent warm and cozy place for her to live. But this situation was one of those things that "just was." There was nothing we could do.

We learned quickly that to leave your flip flops on the porch outside the door was like giving them away. The kids learned to guard their things from whom they had affectionately, and a little fearfully, named "The Old Woman"! On many occasions, I'd wait until she went across the street to eat before sneaking over to her "campsite." I'd put my rubber gloves on and gingerly pull one filthy item out of her bag after another until I'd usually find several pairs of our missing slippers. She found our clothesline as well, and I won't forget the day when ten-year-old Timothy ran into the house wailing, "Mom, she's wearing my favorite shirt!" We chose to "donate" the shirt to her, knowing that by the time she changed her clothes it wouldn't be worth salvaging.

Two-year-old Carolyn learned a lesson in obedience one day when she sneaked out of the house to enjoy the swing on the playground. She knew very well that she was forbidden to go to the playground alone. Nevertheless, the temptation must have been strong, and she succumbed to it. Before realizing that she was gone, I heard Carolyn's blood curdling screams coming from the playground. I hurried to the window and saw her small body writhing this way and that, trying to escape the clutches of the "Old Woman"! She was terrified, and it cured her from sneaking outside alone. For days she told all who would listen, "The old woman tried to get me!" We all got a good laugh out of this. Truthfully, this dear lady was harmless; but she was a frightful sight to a small child.

In July of 2003, we were hit with a powerful typhoon. The rain was torrential, and much of our campus was flooded. At some point the power went out. Late in the afternoon, as our family hunkered together in our home eating Ramen noodles and trying desperately to stay cool, I suddenly remembered the old woman. Tim assured me that her family must have come and taken her home when the storm hit. We decided, however, that we'd better go and check just to be sure. We waded over to the administration building in knee-deep water and found her huddled on the porch. She was curled up into a fetal position, her rice sacks a futile protection against the merciless wind and rain. It didn't take much coaxing to get her inside the building, where we made her a warm bed and gave her some food, towels, and dry clothes. I shudder to think of what we may have found the next day had we not remembered that she was there.

The old woman (we never learned her name) was a permanent resident on our campus for several years. One day, she injured herself and for a time was unable to walk. Only then did her family come and get her. They were able to keep her home, although from time to time she would wander onto the campus.

It never ceased to amaze me that this kind of thing was "normal" – that there was no government agency to sweep in and provide a place for little old ladies like her. It saddened me that families had very little help in caring for their loved ones who suffered dementia or mental illness. Their actions were not meant to be cruel; they simply did not have the means to give the proper care.

Family life was sometimes made difficult by Tim's need to travel. Although it was lonely with him gone, I rarely felt afraid. We were surrounded by a campus family who always looked out for us. One night, however, I learned the meaning of the verse, *"It is better to trust in the LORD than to put confidence in man"* (Psalm118:8).

I was alone with the children during one of Tim's ministry trips when I was catapulted from my peaceful sleep by the crashing noise of breaking glass. I bounded from the bed and, with heart pounding, rushed to the kitchen where the noise seemed to have come from. Shattered glass covered the entire floor in the kitchen, dining, and living room. It only took a moment for me to realize that the glass stove top (one that lifted up when burners were in use) was missing. I was mystified as to what could have caused this. Just then, Valerie and Roanna, having also heard the noise, came running from their room. We all stood there surveying the mess as the girls excitedly informed me that five minutes earlier they had been in the kitchen for a late night snack. They had barely made it back to the bedroom when the glass shattered. I shuddered to think of what may have happened had those girls lingered in the kitchen for a moment more. I thanked God for his protection, spent thirty minutes cleaning up the mess, and wearily made my way back to bed.

It wasn't until the following evening that Timothy Jr., while sweeping the floor after dinner, discovered a discharged bullet in the corner of the dining room. He called to me and, holding the fearsome piece of lead in one hand, excitedly pointed with the other to a perfectly cylindrical, bullet-shaped hole in the ceiling above the table. We realized after some investigation that the bullet had been the culprit for the broken glass the night before. Someone nearby had obviously been recklessly firing a gun into the air (a too-common practice among drunks) and this falling bullet penetrated our steel roof and plywood ceiling, ricocheted off the kitchen table, and zoomed across the room, shattering the stove-top glass and landing several feet away on the floor!

Truthfully, of all the crazy scenarios I ever imagined happening to us while Tim was away, a stray bullet was not one of them. We never did discover who was responsible but recognized God's hand of protection upon Valerie and Roanna from what could have been a tragedy.

OBEDIENCE IS A FAMILY AFFAIR

Missionaries everywhere would agree that the cost of obedience is often brought into sharp and painful focus as the holidays approach. Thinking of all the fun and festivities that were taking place back home left us feeling (especially that first year) very much alone. I well remember our quest to find a Christmas tree. We didn't! After a fruitless search in town, we settled for a small potted plant which sported maybe six or seven fronds. It stood a mere two and a half feet tall, and it took all of one strand of fifty lights to trim it. Valerie, six, and Timmers, two, thought it was grand!

We found that immersing ourselves in the Christmas traditions and activities in our country of ministry did much to ease the pain of being so far away. Filipinos love Christmas and begin hanging lights and playing Christmas music in September. The cutest little ragamuffin carolers would begin showing up in late September or early October. These neighborhood children would loudly belt out their unique versions of familiar Christmas carols while playing various homemade instruments – kitchen utensils, sticks, tin cans, and pretty much anything they could find that would make noise! We were amused and entertained by their nightly serenades, but it became a little problematical when we realized that they expected us to give money in exchange for their musical performance. Eventually we kept large containers of candy by the door, and I think they must have been a bit disappointed to learn that we didn't have a limitless supply of cash. This stemmed the tide of eager carolers a bit after a time.

We began a tradition of visiting someone in need each Christmas Eve. We desired to reach out on this day when we were sorely reminded of how far away we were from our own family.

On one particular Christmas Eve, the night sky was ablaze with the light of a million stars as we made our way down a steep hill and through a rice field and a small grove of mango trees. We were on a mission, our arms laden with gifts of food and clothing for the poor of Casareno.

Although we had been conducting weekly Bible studies there and knew how extremely poor these villagers were, we were not prepared for what we found that night. As we came through a clearing and the small dilapidated houses came into view, a most dismal Christmas Eve picture met our eyes. There were no Christmas lights, no decorated trees, no beautiful clothes, no warm, sugary smells, nor even a hint of joy. Instead, we saw a group of tired, worn, and dirty villagers hovering around one dim bulb that was hanging from a wire above the rough-hewn table where they gambled the evening away. Tired and filthy snotty-nosed children looked on with sad eyes as the adults drank cheap wine, talked loudly, and "celebrated" Christmas. We missionary families quickly explained our purpose for this surprise visit and asked if we could sing. They agreed and stood in awkward embarrassment as we, the "Americanos," began to sing "Silent Night." As we started into the second verse of this well-known Christmas hymn, God's presence came sweetly. I thought – really meditated perhaps – for the first time on those beautiful words as we sang: *"Silent night, holy night, Son of God, love's pure light radiant beams from thy holy face, with the dawn of redeeming grace."* Redeeming grace! **One village woman began to sob. Others became visibly moved. It was as if the light of that love and redeeming grace had broken through the dark, depressing atmosphere and shone into the hearts of these dear, lost people**. They caught a glimpse of the hope that we have because of Christ's coming.

The wonder of the coming of Christ and what that meant illuminated my mind with the real meaning of Christmas. I realized that even I had been lulled into the world's dim view of Christmas. The music, the lights, gifts, food, and even the coziness and warmth of family cannot compare with the simple, and yet powerful, truth. Christ came to bring life and hope to lost, hopeless, sinful, and broken humanity. I felt incredibly privileged that night to have been chosen as an instrument to share the source of that hope.

We felt it important to celebrate the holidays that were distinctly American. And while it would have been easy to send the kids to school on July 4th or Thanksgiving Day, we intentionally made these days special. Most often we would celebrate with other missionary families. Not only were we blessed with wonderful coworkers, but we also had connected with other American and Canadian missionaries from other mission-sending organizations. We'd usually gather during these holidays at the home of the missionary who had the largest house and property, our friends Phil and Rachel Fraiser. They had three children and had been in the Philippines for many years. Rachel was a Filipino by birth but as a teenager had moved to the US, where she met Phil. After college they were married and became missionaries to the Philippines. They lived in a nearby city where Phil pastored a growing congregation. They lived in the house that was Rachel's spacious family home with a large back yard. They also had an outdoor pavilion which was perfect for hosting our missionary gatherings.

These days spent with friends are among our greatest memories. Phil installed a zip line and a rock wall which provided hours of fun for the kids. We'd eat lots of good American food; and afterwards we'd play softball, basketball, or just hang out and socialize. The guys would talk missions, theology, and "guy stuff," while we ladies shared tips on where to find needed items in town and how to make our lives easier living so far from home. Towards the end of the day, Phil would often make a batch of delicious homemade ice cream that we'd all enjoy.

We found that although our denominational backgrounds were varied, we actually had more in common than not. We were united in our love for God and were all living far from home in order to fulfill the Great Commission. The friendships that were forged through these common goals and even difficulties are life-long and some of our most cherished ones.

And so, in spite of what the enemy of obedience assured me would be a family life of unending difficulty, boredom, and one of continuous "missing out," life was, in fact, something very different. Our lives were most definitely not without days of boredom, loneliness, and problems. But there was also, and perhaps in greater measure, a life that was joyful and rich in diverse experiences, amazing relationships, and spiritual reward.

CHAPTER 11

Finding Your Niche . . . in God

The Lord is reminding me in my busyness that the only labor which brings forth eternal fruit is that labor which flows out of love and devotion to Jesus. New debates and controversies are always rising . . . and it's tempting to dive in. Such distractions are nothing but smoke in our eyes, blinding me from the true vision of Christ and his kingdom.
Tim Keep

When we arrived in the Philippines, Tim had a fair understanding of what his initial responsibilities would be. He knew that teaching and mentoring Bible school students would be a primary focus; and in the days to come, other ministry opportunities would open for him, as well. I, on the other hand, felt lost! Aside from caring for my husband and two small children, I had only a vague idea of what my ministry would look like. I felt insecure and unsure of my role. *Where would I fit? Would I be useful in this strange place? What did these dear people expect in a missionary's wife?* I didn't feel at all like a *real* "missionary" – the heroes I had either known or read about. They seemed to have had far more to offer than I.

I learned over time, and through much trial and error, that worries regarding my ministry niche drained me of emotional energy and robbed me of joy. I found that such worries often left me distracted and irritable. I believe that to some degree this restlessness hindered God's ability to work in and through me as he wanted to. Don't misunderstand me. I loved my husband and kids. I love caring for them. Sometimes, however, it felt as if I was doing the same menial tasks in the Philippines that I had done in the States, the difference being that there it was much more difficult and lonely.

I see clearly now that Satan wanted me to believe that being in that foreign land was insignificant and a colossal waste. I did not want this to be true. Little by little, **I learned that if I were to ever find a place of fruitful service and usefulness in God's kingdom, that my *ministry* identity had to come *after* my identity in *God*.** God taught me that I had to first find my "niche" – my security, sense of worth and purpose, and reason to get out of bed each morning – in him and in the person he created me to be. I discovered that when everything I *do* flows from a soul that is anchored in my Creator, then those redemptive works would match the gifts and talents he so lovingly wove into my nature. This discovery was not a painless one, as the following stories reveal.

Upon learning that I could sing, our campus pastor would often arrive at our screen door and announce in his smooth, velvety voice that we would be leaving in five minutes to attend a wedding, funeral, or prayer meeting, and that *I* would be "*rendering* a song"! I remember thinking after a few weeks that I'd never heard the word "render" used so many times in my life, but I just kept *rendering* every time I was asked. Although it was stressful to our "American" minds to have to sing, preach, or pray at a moment's notice, we, in the beginning, acquiesced to all of these demands without complaint. We made a valiant effort to ease into their culture and to prove ourselves worthy of respect.

One of the things that I took note of from the very beginning of our missionary service was the way in which Filipino pastors' wives assisted their husbands in *all* aspects of the ministry. I was especially shocked one Sunday morning when the wife of our local pastor got up and announced that her husband was sick, then opened her Bible and preached a wonderful, anointed message. I mused over the three and a half years that Tim and I had pastored a church in Western Michigan but couldn't recall a single time that I had ever dared such a feat. I shuddered at the mere thought! The efficiency of this lady both impressed and intimidated me.

One day this same pastor's wife came to me and asked me to prepare a message for a Sunday evening service. I recoiled at the question, but then remembered how she had preached for her husband on that recent Sunday morning. I'll pause right here and reiterate that I was a new missionary. I was young, lacked wisdom, and was vulnerable. I could not have her think that I was a "bad" or incapable missionary. I foolishly agreed!

I immediately regretted my decision. As the days passed and the day of my "preaching debut" loomed, I came up with a brilliant plan: *I would have Tim speak in my place!* What a simple solution. I would explain to the dear pastor's wife that my husband would be the "messenger of the hour." It was perfect . . . *until* I shared my plan of escape with Tim. He laughed! He found the whole situation to be very funny, and with a devious grin he told me that he would *not* be speaking for me. In his words, "You have gotten yourself into this situation, and I will not bail you out! You'll have to follow through with your promise." I begged and pleaded but to no avail. I was stuck! I told Tim that he would have to stay home with the kids as I would *not* have him sitting on the front row enjoying my discomfort. He softened a bit and grudgingly agreed to stay behind and babysit. On the day that I was to speak, my apprehension intensified. It was made worse when Tim laughingly threw out his final bit of admonition as I was walking out the door that evening: "Don't yell too loudly or spit too far!"

I don't remember what my message was about that night, and I certainly hope it has faded from the memory of those who were present. I will never forget, however, the invaluable lesson I learned through this embarrassing fiasco. **I never again accepted a ministry opportunity based on intimidation, guilt, or a desire to "fit in" and look good**. I did many things in the ensuing years which stretched me, moved me out of my comfort zone, and increased my capabilities, but only those things that I knew were God's will for *me*. I found that when my gifts were aligned with God's will, then I could count on his enablement and success. To take our ministry cues from those around us – to compare ourselves to others, to measure our worth by their standards and expectations – will always leave us doing unnatural and awkward things! In contrast, we will find that resting in God and waiting for him to open doors will lead to a flourishing, fulfilling, and fruitful life.

Freedom comes when one learns to properly use the two most beautiful letters in the alphabet: N.O. I learned that saying "yes" to good things at the wrong time could be a recipe for failure and disillusionment. I learned to embrace the biblical priority of being mother to my small children and a wife to my busy husband. I learned to be content in this role even while others were scurrying about engaged in what *seemed* to be more important things. I was able to discard the stereotype of what a good missionary looked like. I learned the freedom of leaning into God and seeking to fulfill *his* expectations – expectations much less burdensome than my own.

As years passed, I realized that some of my most powerful ministry moments flowed out of my life as a wife and mother – like the young moms' Bible study I hosted each Friday morning and afternoon. Because Filipino mothers of kindergarteners wait patiently at the school for the duration of the school day, I saw this as a great opportunity to encourage them with the Word and some Christian fellowship. What awesome times we had together studying what it meant to be a godly wife and mother. I gained some great friends and connected with these ladies, not as some lofty missionary, but as a fellow woman endeavoring to care for my family just as they were.

Since I was a stay-at-home mom and always available, I received opportunities on almost a daily basis to practice my nursing skills. My days were always busy and punctuated by frequent knocks on the front door. I spent many hours treating the sick right on my front porch. I dressed nasty wounds, treated skin diseases, removed sutures, looked at throats and infected eyes, and a vast assortment of other ailments. Many I could treat, but I sometimes found it necessary to refer patients to the clinic up the road.

I agreed to be the school nurse for our Bible college and was called upon often to assess and treat sick students. Most of the time these were non-life-threatening situations, and the kids just needed a mom figure to medicate and pamper them a bit to get them through. It was a great way for me to connect with these young people; and it was through these experiences that I realized the importance of teaching a basic health, hygiene, and a first aid class. Many of the men and women studying at our Bible college had come from remote villages; and their unconventional and primitive methods of treating the common cold or a fever were not only ineffective, but often dangerous.

My first middle-of-the-night call to the dorm nearly scared the ability to practice nursing out of me altogether. I arrived after being summoned from my bed by two young students who declared that sister _____ was having a seizure. I hurriedly dressed and followed them and their flashlights through the inky blackness across the campus to the girls' dorm.

I could hear sounds of mass hysteria as I entered the small concrete block structure. We made our way through a common area and into a small room packed to capacity with sympathetic onlookers. The stifling heat in the room nearly took my breath away, and I noticed immediately that the one small window was tightly closed. **My eyes were quickly drawn to the bamboo bed where the sick girl lay.** She was wound into a tight cocoon by several blankets. Her eyes were wide and her nostrils flaring as she desperately sucked in air between her sobs. The girls standing closest to the bed were pressing frantically on her chest. There were others praying loudly, weeping, and denouncing Satan. *I wasn't sure for a moment if I was witnessing an exorcism or just a sick college student!* It took me a moment to assess the whole situation. It was certainly strange and disconcerting to me.

I touched the girl's forehead. She was burning up with fever. I took out my thermometer and was shocked when it registered 105 degrees. Those closest to the bed protested as I began removing the blankets and asked that the window be opened. "Ma'am, you should not remove the blankets, she is chilling!" one student exclaimed. I gently shooed those who were continuing to press relentlessly on the poor girl's chest away from the bed and cleared everyone else out of the room.

I realized that this unfortunate girl, while suffering a virus, was also hyperventilating from the heat, hysteria, and claustrophobia. The soaring temperature in the room, along with the added blankets, was exacerbating a normal fever and causing her to be severely hyperthermic. I believe that without intervention this sweet young woman may have died at the hands of her well-meaning friends. Thankfully, within forty-five minutes she was calm, breathing easily, and her temperature was down to 101. I left for home feeling a bit stressed, having never had so many weird variables thrown into the mix when treating someone with a simple virus. I was also very well aware of the fact that not one person in that dorm agreed with my method of treatment. I realized that to swoop in with my western ways wasn't going to make the superstition magically disappear.

In the ensuing years, I taught many health, hygiene, and first aid classes. This challenged me because I knew that the information I was teaching could prevent so much suffering. It was also daunting, especially when I realized that much of the content was in sharp contrast to what most of my students had ever known about treating and preventing illness. But the Lord helped me to be respectful. I welcomed their questions and enjoyed hearing their stories and methods of curing various ailments. It was so rewarding to hear, much later, from some of those students who went on to pastor churches. I was thrilled to learn that they were using the things I had taught them to help their families, as well as people in their congregations.

Tim and I were awakened one night by loud banging on our living room window. We scrambled out of bed and went to investigate. We found a dear Filipino friend peering desperately through the window. When he saw us, he immediately addressed me: "Ma'am, please come quickly and check my uncle. **I think he's dead, but I'm not sure!**"

We dressed hurriedly and followed him out into the night. There was not a star in the sky. I was thankful for our flashlights as we walked along a winding narrow path to the farthest part of the neighboring village where the "dead" man's family lived. I felt nervous and held tightly to Tim's hand as we passed the snarling dogs guarding each residence along the way. I trembled with trepidation as I walked along, wondering what I was going to find when we arrived. I was pretty sure that my one small medical bag would be no match for *this* situation.

News of the man's misfortune must have spread rapidly in this small village. Even though it was the dead of night, people stood quietly in each doorway, silently watching us as we passed. We arrived and ducked in to a small concrete block dwelling. Just inside the door and to our left was a wooden bed with a man's fully clothed body lying on it. He looked to be about fifty years of age. There were several people standing around the room with worried expressions, while a few stayed outside peering in through the open window and door. I turned my attention to the man on the bed and could see that he was indeed deceased. I had never pronounced anyone dead before and, honestly, felt a bit awkward as this family stood looking expectantly at me. I felt for a pulse in his not yet cold wrist but felt none. I pulled my stethoscope from my bag and listened to his chest for a full minute before straightening up and confirming to the family that he was dead.

We learned that earlier in the evening, the man had complained of chest pain and shortness of breath. He lay down and shortly afterwards stopped breathing. Although our friend, the nephew of this man, was a believer, the rest of the family was not. We spent some time with them that night, sharing comfort from the Scriptures and praying for them. It was our privilege to take part in the nine-day wake for this gentleman and to share the gospel with many people who attended.

I spoke in an earlier chapter of our friend and pediatrician, Dr. Vicky Ang, and of the conversation we had shared in the hospital about partnering together to conduct medical missions. Shortly after that conversation, we returned home for a few months of furlough. While in the States, I spoke to some nursing friends about putting together a medical team to come to the Philippines and help us conduct medical missions in remote villages. I was astounded at the response. Within a few weeks, we had several nurses and others committed to coming the following June. They raised money, not only for their travel expenses, but also enough to purchase needed medicines in the Philippines, which was much more cost effective than buying the same medicines in the US.

The first medical mission was unforgettable! We had our wonderful team from the US and also Dr. Ang, who brought several interns with her. She also brought a surgeon and a dentist, both of whom she had led to the Lord. They radiated with the love of Jesus and, although they lived comfortable, affluent lives in Manila, were willing to ride in our bumpy jeepneys, sleep on concrete floors, and eat simple foods for several days. These worked tirelessly, treating a wide range of illnesses, performing minor surgeries, and pulling hundreds of infected teeth. We, and many of our national pastors, assisted them by screening all incoming patients, giving immunizations, filling prescriptions, and giving vitamins and deworming medicines. We also shared awesome times of prayer and worship as a team each day before the steady streams of people began pouring into the makeshift clinic set up by our pastors and church members. We spent one day in each village before packing up all the medical supplies and moving on to the next. We'd travel by jeepney, often until there was no more road; then we walked, carrying our supplies the rest of the way.

I happened to be seven months pregnant with our fifth child during this first mission. Not only were the jostling jeep rides a challenge, but the final hikes made me (and others) question my sanity. Arriving at one village, Tim was adamant that I not make that final trek, which was a steep and winding hill leading up to the church. He suggested that I ride up on the back of Pastor Francis's motorcycle. Although the thought of this made me a bit queasy and anxious, I agreed to give this a try. I awkwardly situated my larger than normal body into a sidesaddle position behind Bro. Francis. As soon as the bike jolted forward I knew that I had made a mistake! What followed was a terrifying, bumpy, and most uncomfortable fifteen-minute ride up the mountain. We arrived safely, and I spent the next six hours treating patients with the rest of the team.

In the following years, we hosted more teams, which included several American doctors in addition to our Filipino ones, and conducted many more of these missions. We ventured deeper into the mountains to even more remote places. On one occasion, we traveled by jeep for several hours and then walked for two and a half more before arriving at the needy village of Polud. The very last medical mission we conducted demanded an exhausting but exhilarating five-hour hike before arriving at the beautiful village of Caritas. We set up our clinic in the one-room schoolhouse and treated over 350 people. Some of these patients walked more than two hours over the mountain to avail themselves of medical care. I can't quite articulate the sense of purpose and joy that it gave me to work alongside fellow American and Filipino believers to bring hope and healing to so many. More important than even physical healing was the prayer that we offered up for each person who came to us. Many of these received the Lord Jesus Christ as Savior.

If someone would have told me in the earliest, turbulent days of change and culture adjustment that someday I would embrace and love this life and calling, I wouldn't have believed it! We had to pass through some hard, lonely days first. I had to put my feelings aside and learn to trust in the providential leading of God. As I walked in simple obedience and found my identity and purpose in him, he began to broaden my vision, clear my perspective, and bring new and wonderful opportunities before me. If he did this for me, I know he will do it for anyone!

I would love to end the story right here, but honesty will not permit me. In 2009, the Lord very clearly led our family back to the USA and, once again, our lives were turned upside down (a story I may be able to tell later). I found in those days that no matter how long we've walked with the Lord and no matter how many past victories he has given us, when there is a shift in our lives we often find ourselves disoriented and longing for the way things were.

We enrolled our kids in school, Tim began traveling the world for missions, and suddenly I was alone much of the time. My doorbell never rang, those middle-of-the-night emergencies ceased, and I had no big events or teams coming to keep me scurrying about with endless detailed planning. It was cold in the winter; I missed the tropical heat and sun – not to mention my housekeeper, Jesse's tutor, and friends we had left behind. My days consisted of carpooling, packing lunches, doing mountains of laundry, helping with homework, brailling multiple assignments, and cleaning the house. I began to recognize those same feelings of restlessness and boredom. I recognized the stirrings of discontent in this new normal.

It was one afternoon while on my hands and knees cleaning the bathroom floor – that particularly yucky area around the bottom of the toilet – that I had an epiphany of sorts. My phone rang, and I was happy to hear Tim's voice on the other end of the line. He was in Africa, speaking at a pastor's conference; he began telling me of all his adventures there and of the interesting people he was meeting. "Becky", he said, "you'll never guess who I had lunch with today!" He went on to tell me that he had enjoyed a nice lunch and a long chat with Brigadier General Charlie Duke, the tenth man on the moon. Mr. Duke was a born again Christian and was one of the speakers at this conference. I was impressed. We talked for a few more minutes before ending the call.

Afterward, as I continued on with my cleaning, it hit me! *He's having lunch with astronauts, and I'm cleaning toilets! There's gotta be something wrong with this picture!* I almost gave in to self-pity when God spoke quietly to me and reminded me that here again was an opportunity for obedience, that this work I was doing *now* was also a divine calling and privilege. He reminded me of the opportunity he was giving me to embrace and enjoy these quieter days, this change of pace and schedule.

I realized while sitting on my bathroom floor that afternoon that this assignment was just as important as that call to sell everything that I owned and move to the other side of the world. My obedience in this was just as vital to my life and just as pleasing to God. I understood, once again, my assignment was to find my true contentment, purpose, and passion for living – my niche – in, and *only* in God. **I saw afresh that *he must* be my first love and the Fountain of life out of which every blessing and opportunity flows.** I saw that the fruitful life of obedience is a life-long pursuit; and it must never become hard, rigid, and stubbornly anchored in its own place of comfort.

The call to obedience is universal. No matter where you are in this moment of your life, there is a path of obedience for you. I challenge you not to wait for your circumstances to change or become more pleasant and palatable. Do not look over your fence and yearn for the sweeter obedience of your neighbor. Choose to embrace this moment, this circumstance, this lot, this calling, and this relationship for the sake of God's redemptive purpose. I encourage you to take the first trembling step; and you will find, as Tim and I have, that he is already there with all the grace you will need for the next ... and the next ... and the next!

AFTERWORD

God's Amazing Grace for the Obedient

Very recently three of our missionaries and I (Tim) sat in a corner yogurt cafe along a busy, sun-bathed Mexico plaza processing the events of the last two days. Pigeons strutted about on old stone walkways. Pedestrians moved past our window – young couples in love, a family celebrating their daughter's Quinceañera, shoppers hurrying either to or from the market, and citizens out for a leisurely stroll on a beautiful day. In the distance, and in the shadow of an ancient Catholic cathedral, a small youth band played the Mexico national anthem in front of Saltillo's City Hall.

As we went around the table, each one reflecting on the days of strategic planning we had just completed, one of the youngest missionaries, Ivon, offered this profound perspective: "As I listened to all of the discussion over these past two days and as I looked around at our little circle of leaders, it struck me that when God accomplishes his great purpose (and I believe he will), and when in the future a new institute is producing workers for the kingdom, *God will have used broken people to do it!* Not just the brokenness of ... *them*, but the brokenness of *me* as well!"

I was amazed by Ivon's insight. Becky and I have observed that this is how God gets the glory in the lives of his children. **We have** learned that God uses broken men and women who refuse to despair at their own failures or at the failures of others, but who daily *lean* into his grace and who plod on in expectant, joyful obedience. Our family is a debtor to this grace.

In 2009 the Lord clearly led our family back to the USA. Valerie was ready for college, and Timothy was a sophomore in high school. The Lord had provided for Jesse's educational needs for eight years in the Philippines, but Becky and I both felt it was time to avail of State-side technology and resources for the blind and to prepare Jesse for independence. Carolyn and Samantha were still very young, but it was our older children's changing needs we needed to focus on. We had no idea how tough reentry would be for our family and how the Lord would use another season of turbulence to teach us more about his love and faithfulness. Some of these reentry challenges may be written another day, but for now I will only speak briefly of a few of them.

Leaving the church and so many friends in the Philippines was certainly not easy, but we knew that godly leaders were leading the work, that we had finished the work there which God had called us to do, and that we were leaving in obedience.

The greatest challenge for our family in leaving the Philippines was that once again we were being called to sail on turbulent, uncharted seas. Before we boarded the flight for our return, we knew what part of the country we should settle in and where the children would be enrolled in school; but, to be very honest, we had no idea what my work and our ministry would look like after a few months of transition. Nor did we know what home we would live in, how we would possibly afford a down payment for a home, or how we would furnish it once we had it. I rejoice to tell you, however, that in all these uncertainties God provided in amazing ways and without us ever having to say a word – except to him, of course. He provided a home and furnishings. He provided meaningful work and ministry for us. He has provided *every* need and many of our wants. Some of you who read these words are part of the answers to our prayers, and we are so very grateful for your love and kindness.

By far, the greatest challenge we faced upon returning to the United States had to do with the struggle of one of our children. This child's painful struggle caused Becky and me to endure a season of grief like none we had ever endured, including a four-year season of cancer with Jesse. We felt helpless. We questioned ourselves, and sometimes wondered aloud if obedience had been worth it! There were moments when we *felt* abandoned by God and questioned his love and grace. (Perhaps you have been there?) We questioned his promises. In our darkest hour we were *tempted* by thoughts of betrayal, *feeling* that our obedience to God's call should have spared us this family pain. We wondered many days if he still heard and answered prayer.

By the amazing grace of God, we're on the other side of this struggle now and today our family will testify that, "When all around my soul gives way, he then is all my hope and stay. On Christ the solid Rock I stand." Grace held onto our family even in our brokenness! Today, that child is following Jesus, is married to a godly man, and has given us a beautiful granddaughter. God is so good!

Becky and I promised the Lord that if he would make our family whole again, we would never cease to give him the praise he deserves.

Through these reentry trials, the Lord has taught us that while the life of obedience will not spare us *sorrows,* it will provide us a perfect and beautiful *Savior* – one who will not fail to redeem our brokenness for his glory and redemptive purpose in this world. It is our sincere prayer that this strong Savior, Jesus, will be yours today. It is our prayer that he will pour out upon you greater and greater measures of his amazing grace.

Who shall separate us from the love of Christ? shall tribulation, or anguish, or persecution, or famine, or nakedness, or peril, or sword?...

Nay, in all these things we are more than conquerors through him that loved us. For I am persuaded, that neither death, nor life, nor angels, nor principalities, nor things present, nor things to come, nor powers, nor height, nor depth, nor any other creature, shall be able to separate us from the love of God, which is in Christ Jesus our Lord (Romans 8:35, 37-39 ASV).